T H E

SCRIBAL

SOCIETY

The scribal town.

The literate village.

T H E

SCRIBAL

SOCIETY

AN ESSAY ON LITERACY
AND SCHOOLING IN THE INFORMATION AGE

ALAN C. PURVES

State University of New York at Albany

Photographs by Ted Purves

Longman
New York & London

The Scribal Society

Longman, 95 Church Street, White Plains, N.Y. 10601

Associated companies:
Longman Group Ltd., London
Longman Cheshire Pty., Melbourne
Longman Paul Pty., Auckland
Copp Clark Pitman, Toronto

LC
151
.P87
1990

Executive editor: Naomi Silverman
Production editor: Marie-Josée A. Schorp
Cover design: Kevin C. Kall
Cover illustration: From *Silhouettes: A Pictorial Archive of Varied Illustrations*.
Edited by Carol Beranger Grafton. New York: Dover Publications, Inc., 1979.
Text art: Keithley and Associates, inc.
Text photographs: Ted Purves
Production supervisor: Priscilla Taguer

Library of Congress Cataloging-in-Publication Data

Purves, Alan C., 1931–
    The scribal society: an essay on literacy and schooling in the
    information age/Alan C. Purves.
        p.   cm.
    ISBN 0-8013-0378-8
    1. Literacy—United States.   2. Information society—United
    States.   I. Title.
LC151.P87   1990
302.2′244—dc20   89-8346
                                                                CIP

ABCDEFGHIJ-ML-99 98 97 96 95 94 93 92 91 90

For Anne,
who asked me to explain myself

Contents

THE SCRIBAL SOCIETY

CHAPTER 1

The Literacy Crisis
Whose Crisis Is It?

During the 1980s, there has arisen a worldwide cry to eliminate illiteracy in all corners of the globe. It has been announced as a goal of such diverse groups and persons as UNESCO, the United States Department of Labor, Mrs. George Bush, Senator Edward Kennedy, various international companies, and even counties and towns around the world. Attacks against illiteracy are couched in terms that make it sound like a disease that can be cured once and for all. The various proponents of literacy campaigns use medical terminology. They also use economic terminology and see the effects of failure to read and to write as resulting in prison inmates, drug addicts, joblessness, and particularly cost to the productivity of an industrialized or "post-industrial" society. In the United States alone, illiteracy among the adult population is said to cost several billion dollars a year in lost productivity, prison and welfare costs, and adult retraining.

These cries of alarm have become increasingly strident. Why should this be? Why should illiteracy be seen as cognitive AIDS? Why should the fact that a large number of people can barely read or write be so closely tied to the prosperity of an industrialized and thereby urbanized global market economy? I examine a number of reasons in the remaining chapters of this book: They can be summed up in the fact that the global economy—itself a rather recent phenomenon—has become dependent on a cadre of people who can read and write complex texts. (In this book, I use the term *text* to encompass all written language from return addresses to novels to laws.) Earlier economies also depended on the skills of such people, whom I call by the traditional name *scribes*, a term used for those who possessed a special lore

1

concerning written language and who made the flow of goods, religion, laws, and entertainment in and between the towns and cities of the mercantile world easier. Scribes were—and still are—not simply people who can decode and encode written language, or *text*. That ability is a start, but to be a scribe one must have a goodly amount of knowledge about what is to be written, to whom, under what circumstances, and what is intended by the writer of a text that has already been written. This group of people constitutes what I shall call the *scribal society*, a term which I will define in this volume. By so doing, I will elaborate on the complex nature of literacy from a social, epistemological, psychological, and pedagogical perspective.

The ratio of scribes to the total population of any culture in the past has never been very large, although in some isolated and specialized communities such as the Massachusetts Bay Colony or the medieval abbey, it appears that virtually every member who was not somehow brain-damaged was able to read and write. Some societies today brag about high literacy rates, but when one examines these claims closely one finds that such claims are exaggerated. The guideline, such as being able to read a particular religious text, as in Koranic societies, is often met through memorization rather than reading. At the same time, those who claim that 25 million Americans or a similarly alarming percentage of the French are illiterate seem also to be exaggerating. The United States claim is based on the number of students who have not completed a certain number of years of school—either eight or twelve. At times literacy is equated with reading at a grade level on a test, which again is not accurate because the tests are often poorly normed. If one bases the calculation on an extrapolation of the number of applicants who have to take the written part of the driver's test orally because they cannot read the test, the figure drops well below 5 million. It is still a large number, and it does present a social problem in today's society, particularly since a large number of those who are illiterate are also members of minorities and constitute what is called the underclass.

Although the basis for determining literacy has shifted over the past 300 years, the ratio of readers and nonreaders is probably the lowest ever in American history since the time of the Massachusetts Bay Colony. Then the ratio would have been high even if one were to include with that highly literate enclave the several hundred thousand nonliterate Native Americans who surrounded it. One of the triumphs of American education, a triumph matched by other educational systems in only a few other parts of the world, is that it has brought so many people to a moderate level of competence in the scribal society. The vast proportion of American citizens can read the newspaper, write a check, make out a shopping list, and tell whether the mail they receive is "junk" or meaningful. They are not critical readers, and many of them do not read or write very much. There is a smaller group of literate Americans who read and write daily as part of their work, and even as part of their community and leisure activity. These are people who fully subscribe to the tenets of the scribal society and indeed constitute it. Not all of them are members of a professional and managerial class as it is often described, although both groups overlap. Scribes are those who tend to manage our society simply because they have some control of the information and its flow. They create nearly all the facets of contemporary culture. The others are the consumers of that culture. The percentage of scribes in the United States was highest during the middle third of the 20th century. That percentage is on the decline for two contradictory reasons: first, the proliferation of information; second, the disjunction between scribalism and the "good life" of materialism. In this chapter, I explore these two reasons and finally address the implications of the increasing gap both within nations and between nations.

THE NEW SCRIBES
AND THE INFORMATION EXPLOSION

In the last few decades of the 20th century, the world has slipped quietly into a new age that is often referred to as the *information age*. Thanks to various electronic technologies, information can be stored at increasingly fast rates, and more information can be stored than was ever before considered possible. Not all this information is useful to everyone; much of it is relatively useless except to a very few and their interest in the information is for their own intellectual gratification or amusement, as in books of lists or *Trivial Pursuit*. Notice that the term used is *information*, not *knowledge*. As I suggest throughout this volume, the world of text is primarily a world of information, that which is set apart from the people who enscribe it, whether on a cave wall or into the memory of a supercomputer. Knowledge is inside people, information is external to them. Information can be converted into knowledge, a process I explore in Chapters 3 and 4. Texts of various sorts, therefore, are the repositories of information that encapsulate and bolster our individual and collective knowledge.

The amount of information that has been stored has increased exponentially in the 20th century. In the sciences, more has been written in a single decade than has survived centuries of earlier investigation. The sciences have of necessity subdivided to be able to cope with the vast amount of accumulating information. We now have sub-subspecialties in broad fields such as physics and chemistry. A similar fragmentation has occurred in the technical and applied sciences such as medicine or engineering. The social sciences and the humanities have also divided and subdivided.

This fragmentation of fields of information has extended into business and industry as well, so that many companies are highly specialized. Even the large conglomerate has segments whose work is so specialized that their members can barely exchange information about what they do with members of other segments. The only person who sees the whole is the accountant (and perhaps the executive), but even the accountant perceives only a specialized aspect of the whole. There is increasing specialization in such fields as law, advertising, banking, and finance as well.

The publishing industry is well aware of the phenomenon of specialization and has sought to capitalize on it. Although there are many magazines of general interest (most of them newsmagazines that focus on the political and social world), and there are daily and weekly newspapers, a more profitable field for many publishers is the specialty publication that appeals to groups whose interest is particular and whose numbers range from 5,000 to 200,000. Some publishers even seek to secure markets of less than a thousand people who might be interested in such esoteric subjects as hunting wild mushrooms, raising a keeshound, or studying a particular subbranch of ethnomusicology.

Each smaller segment of the scribal society has developed its own forms and conventions of text. Yet each segment has something in common with all the others. There is a variety of scribes, but all scribes share characteristics so that each is a microcosm of the scribal macrocosm. These shared characteristics are the subject of Chapter 2. To some extent each group has its own lexicon; often the same word can mean quite different things depending on the particular group in the scribal society that is writing or reading. Some of these groups use language to maintain an illusion of themselves as separate by virtue of their special knowledge. The physician writes the text of the prescription in an illegible scribble; certain scholarly disciplines develop their own jargon. Sometimes a particular specialized word will move from the narrow field to the general realm of text, as has been particularly true of computer and high finance terms—for example, "interface" and "arbitrage," and people tend to use them metaphorically, much to the horror of the self-appointed guardians of the language. Such terms in specialized contexts are perfectly appropriate. As metaphors they strike many as barbarous.

One reason for the use of specialized vocabulary and syntax in the various divisions of the scribal society is that the members of the "sects," or disciplines, as they tend to call themselves, have established themselves as *inquiring systems*. Such systems develop rules for doing the sorts of inquiry that they want to do and rules for reporting the results of their inquiry to their own members and to the outside world. Thus it is that members of the scientific group who do X-ray tomography develop their specialized language and their specialized kinds of text for their reports to the members of the "in" group of X-ray tomographers. They establish, in effect, a set of conventions for reading and writing that serve to mark the expert from the outsider. By setting the rules for scribal behavior in a particular field, those persons in the field can easily control the entrance of outsiders into that field—perhaps an unfortunate fact of the world of scribes, but a fact nonetheless. The members of a field spend a fair amount of time determining the rules for scribal behavior, and they determine to some extent how the field will be presented to the outside world. In many fields there are groups of translating scribes—otherwise known as "science writers" or "public relations people"—who serve as intermediaries between the scribal specialties and the larger world of the literate. They control the flow and type and form of information that is broadly disseminated.

The translating scribes to some extent also determine what it is important to know about a particular subject as a member of the scribal society as that society is more broadly conceived. In Chapters 3 and 4 I explore a major part of what it takes to be a member of the scribal society, which is comprised of many varieties of knowledge. The knowledge that is deemed both necessary and sufficient for a scribe to have is determined by the scribal society at large, as well as by the subgroups within fields and professions. In terms of literature and what might be thought of as "general cultural knowledge," for example, groups of critics and literary people help determine which authors and texts must be read if a person wishes to be considered really literate. In England, in the 1930s and the 1940s, for example, the critic F. R. Leavis decided that he would seek to change the list of acceptable authors to include certain of the modern—and earlier—writers whom he liked. He and his colleagues undertook a campaign to make a knowledge of the work of such writers as D. H. Lawrence very important to being an English scribe but that of the poet Keats and others less so. Leavis was quite successful in this effort because he influenced people who taught courses in literature at universities and who, more important, made up entrance examinations to those universities. Currently, the American critic, E. D. Hirsch, Jr., is making the same attempt in this country, through the project of teaching and testing "cultural literacy."

In the United States, there are subtle ways of determining the knowledge that constitutes general scribal literacy, the knowledge influenced in part by the extent to which current texts overtly refer to the content and perhaps to the structure and style of earlier texts. A general interest newspaper like *The New York Times* is a good indicator. A typical piece from *The New York Times* editorial page follows:*

Pandora Shamed
Thirteen hundred years ago in Japan, three slender documents—letters? shopping lists? birth certificates?—were placed in a thin box which was then wrapped in brocade.

---

*From "Topics, Time and Money," *The New York Times*, November 7, 1985. Copyright © 1985 by The New York Times Company. Reprinted by permission.

Over the centuries the box was put in three larger boxes, each one of which was wrapped in cloth.

In 1606 the letter box was placed in yet another box and adorned with a covering note. Don't open this, it read, unless you don't mind being tossed out of the Horyuji, a temple in Nara containing the country's oldest Buddhist compound. Eighty-five years later the fourth box was put into a fifth, and the warning was repeated.

This week art scholars who had found the package on the temple grounds opened the fifth, fourth, third, second and first boxes. But did they open the final box? Not on your life. Hadn't the letters said that was a no-no? Instead they X-rayed it, which is how the world knows that it holds three documents.

That, then, is all the world will ever know about that box—and all it needs to know. In putting Pandora to shame, the Japanese have turned what may be three ordinary missives into three extraordinary mysteries.

Aside from the fact that the article deals with a somewhat exotic topic, it is unexceptional to many readers, yet it uses an allusion to Pandora and fails to provide any context for the allusion to help the reader determine who Pandora is and why this action of Japanese scholars might put her (or possibly him or it) to shame. In articles on various topics, the pages of *The New York Times* frequently contain this sort of allusion to Greek and Old Testament mythology as well as to Shakespeare and Dickens and various notable American authors. Clearly, the editors have a set of expectations about their readers, and certainly the expectations differ from those held by the editors of *People* or *Car and Driver*, who tend to use a much more contemporary and specific set of references. Fashion and the interests and memories of various scribal groups determine the cultural literacy of a society like that of the United States.

To be a member of the scribal society today requires general cultural literacy as defined by certain norms as laid down by those who assume that the members of the society or its subgroups share the same world of texts. When the broad population deviates from these norms, it is termed illiterate, not unscribal. That is the case today when those who feel strongly about the norms of scribalism in the "Western tradition" find it challenged not only by the traditions of other cultures but also by the tradition of the new and the tradition of mass culture. For the greater part of society it is probably worse not to know who J.R. is than not to know who J.B. is. For societies other than that of the United States, the situation is similar. Those norms that have provided cultural cohesion and were consonant with the scribal society are being challenged by what has come to be known as *popular culture*. Popular culture has always existed side by side with the culture of the scribal society, yet there was a brief period when the scribal society sought to embrace the popular culture through such vehicles as a common religion or a common set of myths and folklore. As we shall see in the next section, however, this period has ended, because the scribal society has remained with print and the popular culture has moved to the electronic media.

BRAVE NEW WORLD IS HERE

If you have read Aldous Huxley's novel *Brave New World*, you will remember two related aspects of the future society that Huxley predicted. The first was that people were divided on the basis of intelligence tests into various strata, at the bottom of which were people who carried out the routine toil of the society. The second aspect of that society was that all the people were easily gratified through various easily available panaceas—the drink *Soma* and the entertainment called the *Feelies*—so that their sensual and emotional desires were satisfied, and therefore their lives were lives of contentment. It seems to me that both those conditions exist in the industrialized nations. As I have suggested in the previous section, the nature of the information explosion has meant that fewer and fewer persons can be said to be full members of the scribal society. It takes an increasing amount of intelligence and training to pass through the various gates, and even then the potential scribe has a great deal to learn in the workplace about the nature of the activities of reading and writing that must be mastered.

What can one say of the world of the literate? If you walk into a supermarket, you can find a few people working there whose skills at reading, writing, and computation are virtually untapped and disengaged. They do have to know where the bar code on a package is, and they might have to look up the unit price of certain fresh vegetables. They know by the absence of a "beep" when they have to pass the merchandise across the scanner a second time. In some systems they cannot even punch in the fact that the buyer has purchased four of an item; each one of the four has to pass over the scanner. They do not even have to talk to the customer; the machine does that and also tells the customer how much money has been received and how much will be returned. The shopper does not have to be particularly literate either. In this, as in many other "service" jobs, there is little demand that the worker be a scribe, yet such workers can earn a modest wage.

Even the person who has an office job, say as a secretary for a large company, has little need to exercise scribal skills or knowledge. The word processor has a speller (even though it cannot deal with homonyms), it can set up the letter according to the appropriate format, and there is little the secretary needs to do to contribute to the meaning of the letter. In some offices all correspondence is by form letter and is initiated by computer. Newspaper journalists have cut down much of their labor, as have people in all sorts of clerical positions. The machine has enabled them to process more information faster, and because the information that they process is stored automatically, it is easier for others to retrieve it. The complexity of the skills required to operate the new machines diminishes as the machines become more "user friendly." Just as one does not have to think about light and distance to take good photographs, so one does not have to think about many aspects of text in order to produce text. The skills have not become automatic; the demand for their use is simply disappearing.

So it is with many other aspects of life. With today's new banking system, an individual can arrange to have most bills paid automatically by simply having them deducted from a checking or savings account. The system is not too different from that of the old mill town and company store where everything was taken care of for the wage earner—even the thinking about what to do with any earned income. There is little need to be more than just functionally literate in order to transact much daily business.

As for entertainment and the living of the good life, that is purveyed to society by television. Video, movies, and rock music have supplanted the book, the play, and the concert in providing entertainment. Being entertained, even stimulated, has become an increasingly passive process. People do not even need to attend movies or sporting events in person: They can watch them 24 hours a day if they wish, thanks to the videotape and the VCR. The scribal society's vision of a broad populace of readers and writers has all but vanished.

It remains important to be literate, as the majority of people are. One needs to be able to create and receive information that is displayed in the form we call text. Persons who drive, for example, must be able to read the information on signs and maps. It is important also to be able to read labels and directions on packages, to be able to make lists and write checks and fill out various forms. The literate majority can, of course, go to scribes (lawyers, accountants, or notaries) for help with scribal formalities, much as the peasants of India go to letter writers. We could argue that these people are missing a lot, but some of them would disagree with us. They have most of what they want and they can move through life able to secure a good and even an excellent wage, derive a good deal of aesthetic or emotional satisfaction, and participate in many of the societal rituals without having to demonstrate more than the barest competence as readers and writers. They can make meaning of and derive meaning from the world through other media. Their texts are decorative—for example, graffiti, T-shirts, and luggage. That they are manipulated by the scribes and those who produce those media is both a given in their lives and a perennial complaint that they raise, but they usually do nothing about it.

To a great extent these people lead relatively happy and fulfilling lives because the norms of society are focused on physical and monetary resources rather than mental resources. Even in the 1950s, it was believed that the

Environmental text that conveys a feeling more than a message; the misspelling "sez" helps to achieve that reaction.

good life would result from being a scribe. That was a fairly new sentiment for the American society, which had long distrusted scribes and their norms and values, it long being standard practice for Americans to be anti-intellectual. Thanks to the electronic media and to the marketers who purvey material possessions for their own sake, the good life is presented as a world of sensual activity divorced from scribalism. Written texts are no longer the primary means of storing and transmitting information, although the alternative methods continue to use written language. To live the American Dream it is enough to be marginally literate and to have a microwave, a VCR, and the latest car. For many persons, even these material possessions cannot compare to crack, cash, and more crack.

WHERE DO WE GO FROM HERE?
WHAT DO YOU MEAN "WE"?

The first two sections of this chapter suggest that we are currently at a point in the United States and other societies in the industrialized world where two cultures are emerging. These two cultures are not the cultures of the scientist and the humanist or the cultures of the rich and the poor: They are the scribal culture and the mass culture. In a sense, we have arrived at a position similar to the one that existed in many parts of the world up until the middle of the 18th century—the point at which the middle-class literate society emerged, and literature flowered. The flowering lasted for 200 years. There was a peasant or worker or serf culture underlying this broadly scribal culture, but the hope was that the "less adept" culture would diminish and that even the working class would join the ranks of the cultured. It was for this reason that Workingmen's Institutes and village Literary Societies were established. Now we appear to be entering an age of scribal "meritocracy" and literate peasant class.

The flowering of music, art, and literature that began in the 18th century appears to be withering in part because of the tremendous increase in information and the consequent need to learn more in order to be a scribe. The withering has resulted also from the fact that achievement of the good life no longer is based on being a scribe. Popular culture is dominant. To be good, honest, and especially to be rich, one does not need a high degree of scribal lore. The scribal society is still crucial to the functioning of the world economy, but it is no longer thought necessary and perhaps not desirable for everyone to join that society.

Such is one gloomy picture of the future: a society of two separate cultures. Will that prophecy be fulfilled? I cannot answer that question fully. Many of the forces that control society, the forces represented by commerce and advertising, are seemingly quite happy with that possible outcome. They

Shadows of the new world of text.

have no trouble with a world in which *People* magazine provides the index of cultural knowledge and of literacy, a world in which a relatively few control access to the scribal culture by the many. There is the remote possibility that many members of the mass culture will become dissatisfied with their lack of access to scribal culture and will want to become scribes themselves. The emerging economic and social picture of the industrialized nations is such that literacy will be the province of the many but scribalism the province of relatively few. At the same time, the sense of powerlessness of the merely literate may come to outweigh their contentment with their lot. In that case, it is possible that more and more people will be willing to embark on the road to scribalism and seize control of information. It has happened in the Third World. It could happen here.

In the succeeding chapters of this book I explore first the history of scribalism, then its epistemology and its psychology. Finally, I set forth a curriculum for our schools that might help more children become scribes.

CHAPTER 2

The Scribal Society
from the Dordogne Valley
to Silicon Valley

Near the dawn of human time, someone somewhere made a mark on a piece of stone, a wall, or some dried mud. The mark had a purpose. It was to help the person remember something. What was the thing to be remembered? When did this happen? Where did it happen? No one knows the answer to these questions exactly. For a long time it was thought that the first occurrence of this sort of marking was in Mesopotamia about 2000 B.C. and that the purpose of the marks was to record the price of some goods or their quantity or destination. Recently, that date has been pushed back 10,000 to 12,000 years to the caves in southern France that were the home of Cro-Magnon man. It has been suggested that these early marks formed some sort of lunar calendar.

Wherever the origin of writing, it is one of the earliest inventions of the human race, occurring perhaps shortly following the development of simple tools and perhaps at about the time that it occurred to someone that rolling was easier than carrying. Writing was not the representation of natural language, the way we now think of writing, but one of a number of symbolic creations of humankind along with dance, drawing, and song. Eventually people came to realize they could use a variety of marks to indicate concepts and objects and even to imitate spoken language through a phonemic transcription system.

Even in its earliest stages of development, written language existed apart from the oral language by which people shared their ideas and feelings, their fears, and their concerns about the future. Written language did not come into existence for such communal purposes; it was only a way by which a person

An example of ancient cuneiform writing, circa 3000 B.C. (From *Sumerian Tablets in the Harvard Semitic Museum* by Mary I. Hussey. Cambridge, MA: Harvard University Press, 1912. Reprinted by permission.)

could record some important piece of information for retrieval at some later time. It had to fulfill two demands: It had to be accurate and clear, and it had to be unchanging. Archeological remains indicate that much of this information was arithmetic in nature; it involved numbers of days, of loads of barley, of camels or donkeys, or prices. Later it was found to be a useful means of storing other sorts of information, such as laws or the names of people, events, or places. With writing came the idea of recording information for later retrieval.

This is not to say that oral language did not have similar uses. People did use oral language as a means of retaining certain kinds of knowledge and information, but the two forms differed sufficiently so that writing soon became the more successful tool for the storage of much of what people wanted to retain. It also was used to store relatively useless information as well. Quite early in the history of writing someone marked a name on a cliff-face, and graffiti entered history.

The efficiency of writing for storing information is obvious. Once marked down, the marks remain unchanged until they are erased by human or natural forces. By making a mark on a surface, one can transform an idea or a piece of information into something physical that transcends time and space. To say something aloud, such as "Five bundles of wheat," is to commit that vocalization to airwaves that theoretically could travel forever through space. Practically, however, they do not, and the utterance is lost. Speech is evanescent and temporal. Written language is spatial, visible, and durable.

Since its invention, writing has evolved considerably, and a number of aspects of that evolution may be distinguished. First, it is clear that there have been changes in the surfaces on which people wrote and thus in the instruments used for writing. The transition from stone or damp clay marked by the stylus or stone point to papyrus or parchment marked by the brush was a major change that allowed the marks to become curved rather than angular. The development of paper and permanent inks prolonged the life of many documents, and the printing press and the cheap production of paper had profound effects. The primary effect of the printing press was to make possible the multiplication of copies of any text. In the 1960s, the photographic copying machine changed the world of text by making possible the proliferation of copies in a way not previously conceivable. Today, as a result of electronic technology, writing can be stored in forms different from the written or printed page (now known as "hard copy"), the existence of which earlier was axiomatic. The word processor, and, perhaps even more important, the copying machine have altered our very conception of such terms as *publish* and *text*.

A second major change in the nature of writing is the change in distance a text may travel. Early written texts appear to have stayed within a relatively small area, bound by the language and by the limitations of travel and communication. Today, a text can appear simultaneously at many points on the globe. The distance that texts have traveled in time is even greater than the distance in space. We have access to texts produced as long ago as 3000 B.C. Such a transport across time through language is possible only with some means of recording the language. Written text has been a particularly effective mode of recording, even though today we do not always know what it is that the ancient scribes were writing despite the fact that we can see the text. We have lost the key to the code.

A third major change in written language involves the nature of the information that is stored. No longer is the information only commercial data, although commercial writing still accounts for the lion's share of what is produced as text. In addition, we have laws and rules, directions, historical documents, advertisements, and the records of people's thoughts and feelings concerning almost everything under the sun as well as beyond the solar system itself. Not only has the quantity of information burgeoned in the past 5,000 years; its variety has as well. This change in the nature of stored information has brought with it a change in the uses to which being able to read and write are put. We no longer read and write simply to get or put down information for some commercial purpose. We read and write in order to learn, to inform or become informed about the world, to convince others or to allow ourselves to be seduced, to express our feelings or to relax, to provide for others, to have an aesthetic experience, or simply to keep in touch with one another. All these uses tend to complicate the state of being literate. We now use written language for all the functions of oral language. Yet the reason for writing remains the same—to record the information so that it can be retrieved at some later date.

The fourth change in writing is a necessary consequence of the first three. The means of production of writing, the distance and speed with which writing can be transferred, and the kinds and uses of writing have multiplied. So, too, has the economics of writing: Writing has become a major industry. Among the early instances of writing was an "envelope" of clay around a clay ball. The mark on the "envelope" indicated what was on the ball and therefore what the ball signified. Presumably someone made the balls and the clay envelopes. Was this the first stationery manufacturer? In the ancient Egyptian civilization, the business of being a scribe, a person who could read and write, was a fairly lucrative one. Whether the scribes also manufactured their quills and papyri is unknown, but certainly they did fairly well at the scribal trade, well enough so that it was a desirable profession. In other societies, the scribes were slaves, but it was a slavery that carried with it certain perquisites. As the machinery of writing developed, it was clear that there was money to be made in it. The printing press was not developed in the 15th century merely as a venture in pure exploration. The fact that Gutenberg was forced into bankruptcy by the people who had helped him to establish his press shows that they realized a good deal of money could be made through the sale of Bibles, calendars, and other kinds of writing. As the means of production became easier, it was important for persons producing writing and texts to find new markets. Literacy was tied to a person's financial rise and entry into the middle classes, and it was not long before printers and publishers saw that the spreading of literacy would help them get more customers and therefore make them richer.

Since the development of the printing press and later with the development of the powered press, printers have continually sought new markets through the advertisement, the almanac, the cheap book for a quick sale, the newspaper, the magazine, the "how to" book on all sorts of topics, and various sorts of commercial papers. They have also found new markets in readers of various sorts: the child, the yearning maiden, the antiquarian, and the prurient, for example. These groups have become subdivided even more so that there are now special markets for all sorts of books and magazines. These markets have often brought with them new demands for such items as illustrations and colored inks, paper that reproduces with high quality, and paper that is almost disposable after a single reading. The technical developments are myriad, and they have spawned a number of ancillary industries to the printer such as the paper manufacturer, the press manufacturer, the graphic designer, the binder, and the manufacturers of all the various sorts of paraphernalia that fill stationers' and office supply shops. The literacy industry has accounted for several nations' emergence from backward farm societies to modern industrial ones: Finland and Canada for wood pulp and Singapore for printing are but three examples of societies that have profited by the need for increasing numbers of people to have access to text and the means of producing it.

As writing became one of the major industries, it created a subsidiary industry that is involved in making more people literate: the school. I explore that industry in Chapter 5. For now, it is enough to say that literacy and scribal education are a major aspect of any nation's education budget and that many private industries around the world devote their whole energy to teaching people to read and write at either a level of basic literacy or at the advanced level of being a scribe, and they appear to make a substantial profit at so doing. Added to this industry is another that studies literacy and writing and reading. Scholars look at literacy philosophically, historically, psychologically, economically. Entire departments at universities are devoted to the contemplation of this invention and its consequences.

Against the four facets of the evolution of written language from a somewhat simple tool for the recording of information to a highly complex network, there remain an equal number of constancies, or persistent threads, by which we may say that the first written text, that set of marks on a stone in southern France, is linked to what you are reading at this moment, despite the fact that one was painstakingly chipped at with one stone against another and the other was composed on a word processor. The first thread is the functional one of storage against time and space; the second is the thread of the spatial arrangement of symbols; the third is the conventional nature of texts and their uses; and the fourth is the way by which the first three set apart the users of written language into a special group—the scribes—that we call *cultured*. In the rest of this chapter, I explore those four threads in some detail.

SETTING IT DOWN AND GETTING IT STRAIGHT

Although we do not know what inspired the first writer, there appears to have been a need to remember something by making a significant mark on some surface. Such an early writer knew or planned what the mark would signify, so that when the writer returned to the stone he or she remembered its meaning. Subsequent marks could have been added to the first to indicate a series. Each day, the writer could return and "read" the marks and realize that they had remained unchanged. Presumably, their meaning for the writer had remained constant as well. The stone had stored the information for the writer.

That is a remarkable fact. A person could come back to the stone again and again, and the marks would still be there. Later, the marks took on more and more complex symbolic structures, but the fact remained that no matter how complex the organization of the symbols and the spaces, once the marks were placed there, they remained. They might fade, and some forms of writing were more durable than others. But the symbols persisted. You may shut this book now, put it away for a month, and come back to this page and find the same marks & # " ˆ(> right where they were when you left them. Whether the marks will "mean" the same thing a month or a year from now is another matter, one that I take up in Chapter 3. But the marks remain. The information has been stored, and it can be retrieved.

Let us consider what this fact about written text implies. What does it mean to have something called a text to which we can refer at will with the surety that it will be as it was when we last looked at it? In the first place, it frees the memory. No longer do people have to remember great amounts of knowledge. All they need remember is the coding system and the principles for encoding and decoding the knowledge—turning it into information. As we shall see in the Chapter 4, this burden of memory is not relieved to the extent that one might first think. The various aspects and conventions of written texts have become so complex that to be able to read a volume like this requires having a great deal of information. The amount that we have to store in our brains to read the multifarious texts that come across our ken is large, but it hardly equals the amount of knowledge that we would have had to store were there no written language. Our minds are free for other things; text can store more information than any one person could possibly know.

More important for a group of people in a village or a region, the same piece of information can be passed from person to person without being changed through the vagueness of oral memory. There is a familiar psychological experiment that is also a party game in which the first in a chain of people utters a sentence; then the sentence is repeated from person to person along the chain. It usually returns to the original speaker quite garbled. The fact that the message is written insures that it will make the voyage along the chain relatively less damaged than an oral version.

By being encoded and immutable, the written text assumed a role in society different from that of oral language and thereby changed the very fabric of society. This role of text has been studied by anthropologists and psychologists as well as by literary critics and historians. Certain changes in the nature of society took place as consequences of the development of written language. One change was the possibility of commerce with larger and larger areas of trade. Written messages could accompany travelers, and goods could be shipped over longer distances, depending of course on the quality of the transport service. Together with a coinage, or monetary system, written language served to spread trade and capitalism. As both became more sophisticated, the spheres of trade encompassed the world.

Historians and anthropologists have suggested that other major changes in society have resulted from the advent of text. Among them are changes in law that provide a secular rule that does not entirely depend on force. Rather, written law, or text, carries with it the implicit threat of force. When there is a taboo or a custom in a society, the weight of either may remain relatively constant over time, but either may dissipate because emphasis may be changed as it is passed orally from person to person or generation to generation. Written law has the advantage of always being available for reference. The codes of Hammurabi and Napoleon were relatively static and could be used as a set of guiding principles not unlike the constitutions of countries, clubs, and other organizations. These constitutions and laws can be referred to at any time by the literate members of the society, and they can settle disputes or even raise them.

If the advent of writing brings secular law, it can also advance or change religion. The strength of the world's great religions lies in their having texts as their authority. When Moses ascended Mount Sinai and brought down the tablets with the Ten Commandments, he not only established a set of laws; he also enabled those laws to exist within a religious context. The text presumably came from a divine hand; it was both law and the assertion of divine power through the permanence of text rather than through the inspired preaching of an individual or through some other transitory miracle. Similar assertions can be made concerning the Koran, the Gospels, the *Baghavad Gita*, and the writings of Buddha, Lao-tze, and Confucius, as well as the texts of various lesser religious and quasi-religious figures. The text itself is important as a vehicle for spreading the religion, but more, the text itself becomes sacred. The history of Islam is instructive in this respect, for it is known that after the revelation to the prophet and later, his death, the impulse was to spread the religion orally. People went to great lengths to memorize his sayings, but they soon found that they were losing them, so they used various bits of bark and other materials on which to jot notes. It was decided that it would be best to have a copy of the whole text that could remain the same throughout the growing Islamic world. The decisions about the particular writing system and the various conventions were momentous ones, and once they were settled so was the shape of the text, which has remained the same to this day. More important, perhaps, the text is one of the few current religious texts that has not changed its language; those who would follow Islam must learn Arabic. The early versions of many of the world's great religions saw the text itself as sacred (a phenomenon we explore further in Chapter 3) and therefore available only to those who were properly trained to use it. Judaism, Christianity, Hinduism, Buddhism, and Taoism all started this way. In the West, Martin Luther caused a great revolution by suggesting that the Bible could be translated into the vernacular and that each reader could be his or her own priest. Most contemporary religions have allowed adherents to read the text in a translation, but the very physical text of the Koran is sacred and close to immutable in surface and substance. It is this view of text that has led the Ayatollah Khomeini to call for the death of Salman Rushdie and his publishers and printers. To him, the palpable text of *The Satanic Verses* is blasphemy.

Like the secular code, the religious text has enabled large groups of people to come together and to have something in common. The texts have been variously interpreted, and people have treated them quite differently. Each in its own way has enabled disparate peoples to join a community across space and throughout history, however.

The fact of information storage in the form of written documentation has meant other things to society as well. It has given people a history, a record of their past. Because they have a recorded history, they can have a renaissance, or rediscovery, of the past. Information storage has further meant that people have had access to different histories, or different versions of the same event, and have been able to compare them in order to arrive at "the truth." Written language and the storage of information have enabled people to have records of earlier constructions of the world and have thereby enabled such fields as science to exist. (Science has a special relation to written language, as we shall see in the next section.) The record that writing has given us simply by virtue of its ability to preserve information includes primarily narrative information—that is, records of events and participants in events, but also descriptions of peoples, places, things, and ideas.

This invention has not always brought blessings with it. Sometimes information storage and the possibility of verification and reference have brought libel and slander, as well as censors who have limited what was printed or distributed and persons who have falsified information.

Of course there was no need for the information to be "true" in that the peoples, places, or things really existed or that the ideas corresponded with perceived reality or had to be logical. Writing was early used to store the products of the imagination. It provided the script of a drama, the record of a song, or an epic such as *The Iliad*. Once these songs, plays, and tales were set down, there began to be a "correct" version, an issue discussed in the next few pages. The fact that such material could be written, however, did much to change the form of poetry, drama, and tales. It was no longer necessary to have some sort of mnemonic device such as certain kinds of repetition to aid memory. Because the reader could go backward and forward in the text, the writer could create complications of plot that were almost unthinkable in oral forms of storytelling. It has been argued that the very existence of the modern novel resulted from the combination of the printing press and the rise of a reading public.

Another aspect of information storage is that the information accumulates. A writer can set down a story. That story does not have to be rewritten but becomes a text to which the next storyteller can refer or about which a commentator can write a series of remarks. The commentator or the next storyteller can refer to the first story and send the reader to it, or if the reader has already read it, the reference becomes mental. In this way subsequent texts can refer to earlier texts or can incorporate bits and pieces of them. The information in a text, then, can include information from or about earlier texts. Over time, annotations, glosses, footnotes, critical and authoritative editions, and explanations and criticisms accumulate. The whole edifice of texts piled upon texts thus becomes a massive accumulation of information.

All these various uses to which writing has been put have in common that they tend to make permanent (or at least more permanent than the oral version) the information that the writing encodes. One of the consequences of this fact, and the attendant fact that people return to the text looking for the same information, is that the idea of accuracy is associated with text, especially accuracy of the information contained. Even more important is the accuracy of the recording of the information. If more than one document about the same piece of information is written, the chance of error is immediately introduced. In the days of scribes and copyists, there was always the chance of the "slip of the pen," or the careless omission or addition. In printing, such errors constantly occur, in part because of the speed with which the printer works. Today, when there are computer compositors and programs that edit and check spelling, one constant problem is the fact that the editing program cannot detect a homonym or an error that also makes a correct word.

Concern with the "correct text" created a new occupation: editor, a person who was not the scribe but who checked the work of the scribe or the

Chaucers Words unto Adam, His Owne Scriveyn

Adam scriveyn, if ever it thee bifalle
Boece or Troylus for to wryten newe,
Under thy long lokkes thou most have
the scalle,

But after my makyng thou wryte more trowe;
So ofte a-daye I mot thy werk renewe,
It to correcte and eek to rubbe and scrape;
And al is thorugh thy negligence and rape.

Chaucer's curse of Adam the scrivener.

copyist. As with the invention of written language itself, no one knows who the first editor was. At some point, when enough versions of a text existed, a different sort of editor appeared, one who checked the various versions and decided which was the correct one. Both sorts of editor are still very much in evidence.

It is possible that the very existence of a written version of people's thoughts and observations also helped bring about a concern with the "accuracy" of the information in the text and the form of the text itself. That is a matter of conjecture, but some persons argue that the fact that observations can be recorded means that they can be verified. The idea of comparing two different versions of an event was certainly made easier when one had texts of those versions and could make scrupulous comparisons.

LOOKING AT THE LAYOUT

As you look at this page, and you have to look at it in order to follow my train of thought and even to criticize, accept, or reject it, there are certain features of the page that are crucial to written language but that are too often overlooked. In addition to its being stable in that the marks remain when you close the cover and come back later to the page, the page is in the same place, because of the book's binding, and you can return to it easily because it is numbered. Third, the page has a pattern that resembles other pages you have seen so you know how to look at it in order to do that thing we call *reading*.

The conventions of our language—the visual compacts between writer and reader—require that the marks be arranged in horizontal rows. They can be made meaningful if you start at the upper left corner and go through each row from left to right until you come to the bottom right corner. Then you go to the next upper left corner. There are other aspects of this compact. Larger marks indicate either a beginning or something that has a particular importance. A blank indicates the end of a unit, and the larger the blank the bigger the break between units and perhaps the greater the difference between the units. Each of these conventions evolved over a long period, as did the compact that established the meaning of the individual marks and combinations of marks.

Most of the conventions of written language were arrived at by those who made it their business to produce and receive text, the scribes: monks, copyists, scriveners, rubricators, printers, and editors. Many of the conventions resulted from the best compromise they could make given the materials they had to work with. When writing was done with stone incising stone or wood, the best way to make marks was in straight lines. When there became available a surface such as parchment and brushes or some other instrument with which to make the mark on the surface rather than incising it, curved symbols became possible. The vertical writing system of the Chinese appears to have come about because the writing surface was a piece of bamboo. It was easier to go down and then repeat the process rather than to go around. Once such conventions get started, they are hard to change.

As the means of writing became routinized and widespread in a society, a certain uniformity in the formation of the various characters was effected. Standards for the production of such characters, whether they were hieroglyphic, ideographic, or alphabetic, emerged and a "classic hand" tended to set the pattern. In some societies, such as Japan in the 11th century A.D., the elegance of one's calligraphy became a mark of breeding and, in women, a sign of desirability. In Europe at about the same time, the beauty of the illumination of the initial letter of a text was treasured. Early printed books were unpopular unless the printing looked like the work of a copyist. Later, printed texts came to be judged by their own standards, including the style and elegance of a type font. Today some people spurn text that has been produced on a word processor and printed with a dot-matrix printer because the text is not "letter-quality," following the premise that text is finer if it is produced on a typewriter. For centuries people have judged texts by their physical appearance, and this judgment of the text has been an implicit judgment of the character of the person responsible for the text, whether that person be the actual producer of the copy or the supposed originator of the text.

The physical appearance of a text, then, results from a concern for uniformity in the use of the various signs and other visual conventions and from the desire of those who produce and receive texts to have the result be, if not attractive, at least not unpleasant to look at. The desire for uniformity was clearly apparent in the early days of printing in Europe, when a great deal of attention was devoted to the creation of legible fonts. This activity led to the acceptance by printers in a number of languages of the font that we now call Roman. Its only rival was the Gothic typeface used in Germany and the Nordic countries, which was able to hold its own for more than three centuries, in part because of the strength of Lutheranism and in part because there was sufficient international printing commerce within that group of nations. Russian and Greek printers kept their orthographic systems as well, but they had fairly early reached typographical standards acceptable to the rest of the world. The experience of the European languages is matched by that of other writing systems, particularly those written languages (such as Chinese and Arabic) that became extensive early in their history. Both Chinese and Arabic developed standards of calligraphy and pointing or the marking of vowels and intonation patterns that have persisted and are still the rule.

Uniformity is not the only factor in the physical design of a written language. Other aspects of a visually based system of recording information give the design unique properties. One of these is that items can be arranged in groups in two-dimensional space. Various items can be set with each other, and placing them in adjacent rows or columns signals that they are grouped. Thus one can make lists, but more important, can indicate through arrangement an order or a system to the list. Lists and catalogues are possible in oral language as well, but the possibility of arranging information in space so that the arrangement itself indicates meaning has led to a number of extraordinary mental products, such as acrostics, anagrams, cryptograms, and crossword puzzles, many of which we take for granted. With a visual arrangement, one can make cross-references and note repeated sequences.

Perhaps the two most frequent sequences are the ordered list and the cross-tabulation; the telephone directory and the calendar are the most ubiquitous exemplars of these two kinds of arrangement of information in two-dimensional space. The telephone directory is an example of a sequence in which the arrangement of words is controlled on the basis of initial symbols. In alphabetic languages, this system is relatively standard, despite some minor variations in the presence or absence of certain letters and differences in the pronunciation of the letters. Recently, the format of the directory has been further standardized so that different colors of paper serve as a clue to what will be found where in the book. Thus, without being adept at the language, a visitor can come to a city and, knowing the spelling of a name but otherwise ignorant of the language, be able to find the desired number in the telephone directory.

The progression of type fonts shows the move away from a manuscript style toward legibility. Top left: Aesop's *Fables* translated into English and printed by William Caxton in Westminster, 1483; top right: types used by Hentzsken, Berlin, 1578; bottom left: roman and italic types showing "modern" tendency, Cecchi, Florence, 1691; bottom right: Giambattista Bodoni, *Manuale tipographico,* first edition, Parma, 1788. (From *Printing Types: Their History, Form, and Use* by Daniel Bradley Updike. Cambridge, MA: Harvard University Press, 1922. Reprinted by permission.)

The calendar can be thought of as the epitome of the table. It is based on what is conjectured to be the Cro-Magnon use of a marking system, the division of time into uniform periods, that we referred to in Chapter 1. These uniform periods operate in a system of cross-references, the first of which is the basic unit, the day, that is, the period from sun to sun. Days are also arranged into two recurring blocks, one of which is related to the lunar cycle, the other of which is a shorter sequence between holy days or days of designated rest. The arrangement of these units is best shown two-dimensionally. Between cultures there may be differences such as which day is designated at the beginning of the shorter sequence, and the length and division of the longer sequences. Some calendars may reverse the axes from the normal display, but the principle of the two-dimensional grid is common.

The fact that a text can display information in two dimensions is more important than its application in the calendar. In societies that move from top left to bottom right, writers arrange material to make use of or to surprise that normal expectation. In making use of the expectation, writers may prepare charts secure in their knowledge that they will be read in that downward diagonal way. With the addition of various lines and arrows, they may make even more complex diagrams, maps, and charts so that people may symbolize sets of relationships both real and hypothetical in two-dimensional space. These additional uses of the space are but elaborations on the basic format of the calendar, just as various sorts of lists, tables, and indexes are but elaborations on the telephone directory.

These are but two of the visual elements of written text. Both are the product of extensive evolution, and both have become conventions in the display of text. There are other visual conventions as well, many of which appear to transcend language and culture or even orthographic system:

- The SIZE OF THE TYPE is generally seen as an indication of a word's importance or lack of it.
- The **darkness of the text** is another indication of its importance, as may be the use of a second or even a third or fourth color, as in the rubric or redletter text that may appear beside the main black text.
- A variation in the angle or shape of a segment of text (*as in the use of italic*) can indicate the importance or lack thereof of the segment.
- The placement of text on the page can indicate either the type of text or give a clue as to its meaning or purpose.

The visual arrangements of words on a page were selected for various reasons: to readily identify the sender of a letter, to place the ingredients in one place, to make the text more compact and thus more easily carried by a priest, and to save paper. Some scholars have even suggested that the sonnet

The form and place of these texts convey the message even without legible letters.

became so popular in Renaissance Europe because it was very close to being square when printed. Certainly it allowed a whole poem to appear on a single page.

As various type fonts have come to be associated with certain kinds of text, so the type font has come to have its own symbolic force even when transferred to another context. Writers and artists over the years have come to use these various visual aspects of text to help make their meaning, as shown by the poems by George Herbert and Evoen Gomringer. In some cases, the writer has used a combination of text and illustration or has used the format

---

THE ALTAR

A broken A L T A R, Lord, thy servant reares,
Made of a heart, and cemented with teares:
      Whose parts are as thy hand did frame;
      No workmans tool hath touch'd the same.
            A H E A R T alone,
            Is such a stone,
            As nothing but
            Thy pow'r doth cut.
            Wherefore each part
            Of my hard heart
            Meets in this frame
            To praise thy Name:
      That, if I chance to hold my peace,
      These stones to praise thee may not cease.
Oh let thy blessed S A C R I F I C E be mine,
And sanctifie this A L T A R to be thine.

—George Herbert

SILENCE

silence silence silence
silence silence silence
silence   silence
silence silence silence
silence silence silence

—Gomringer

Two poems: "The Altar" by George Herbert, and "Silence" by Evoen Gomringer. ("Silence" is reprinted by permission from *The Book of Hours and Constellation*, translation by Jerome Rothenberg. Hastings-on-Hudson, N.Y.: Ultramarine Publications, 1968.)

to illustrate the text. In other cases, the writer has used visual features as a sort of pun.

Finally, artists and writers have fused text and illustration for centuries, at least as far back as the early hieroglyphic wall paintings of Egypt, the Chinese scrolls, and the Mayan temple decorations. The idea has been carried on through the Bayeux tapestry, the illuminated manuscript, the work of William Blake, and down to the present-day picture book and comic book. The artist–writer has the ability to force the reader's eye to suspend its motion or speed up as it goes through the pages of a book, to force the reader to attend to a certain part of the page or frame within a page, to create narrative or dramatic effect by use of visual marks on the page.

All these examples, which are but a few from the history of written language and texts, suggest that the visual presentation of information is of great importance to writers and readers. Many people will look at a draft and say, "It doesn't look right." Others will know that a particular part of what they are writing "needs more space." These spatial and visual approaches to text complement and supplement those approaches that consider the semantic relationship of mark to meaning. The visual aspects of a text are part of the text's semantics. They help writers to store the information in the desired manner, and they signal to the reader how the information is to be retrieved and understood. By using an alphabetical list, for example, the writer avoids seeming to award prominence to any one item of the list. Curiously enough, few who discuss the nature of writing and texts pay much attention to this most obvious feature of the medium—its appearance.

Yet even the child just beginning to read and particularly to write is well aware of what is going on when pencil is put to paper or keyboard to screen. The look of writing and the fusion of writing and the visual symbol are readily apparent in the writing of young children. Many a child has sought to a make a rebus of her name, and believes that she is writing a meaningful message because she has shaped the marks to resemble the spacing of text, or has experimented with various colors and fonts in composing her earliest messages.

It is precisely because of its two-dimensional symbolic capacity that writing has enabled people to create certain kinds of order out of the world around them. We have the calendars and the directories that we do because we use a two-dimensional system. That system has also enabled us to create the world of mathematics and science. The equation $E = MC^2$ is possible only because we have top and bottom and left and right on the page. Although other kinds of human knowledge were made possible because information could be stored, our scientific and technical success as well as our prospects for mass self-destruction are made possible because we can display symbols and the concepts they represent in two-dimensional space.

THE CONVENTIONAL WISDOM
OF WRITTEN LANGUAGE

Without really thinking about it, you could tell that you were about to begin a new section of this chapter. You could do so because the use of a larger-than-usual space between lines and the boldface lines of capital letters are two of the normal ways to indicate that a new section of any piece of writing is about to begin. This is but one of the aspects of the layout of a written text that has come to take on a conventional meaning. If I were to use this same convention in the middle of the paragraph, you would rightly treat it as a violation of a compact. Layout and the physical format of the text, however, are but parts of what has become conventional about written language. These conventions are a necessary consequence of the creation of a tool that allows one person to store some desired idea or piece of information so that any one of a number of people anywhere else can have access to it. These conventions allow for some variation or deviation, but to go too far is to violate the convention.

Among the earliest conventions of written language were the symbols themselves and the order, number, and shape of the symbols that were necessary to convey a particular piece of information. It became clear to the early scribes that if they were to use written language to transmit information to some unknown or distant person, it would be necessary to adhere to some conventions as to spelling and word order.

Conventions in language are not the exclusive property of its written form. Oral language also has its conventions and formulaic expressions, such as the common phonemic structure of a language or dialect, a common grammar, and the structure of stories, songs, and jokes. The conventions of oral language in a culture also include its taboos—what one does *not* say. As with the conventions of oral language in a society, so the conventions of written language are manifestations of an elaborate social code that is available to every full member of a particular culture. The more complex and specialized the literate culture, the more complex are its conventions. At the same time, conventions of literate culture enable individuals to move across the dialectic or linguistic boundaries that would have separated oral cultures. Such was the case of written Chinese which, by virtue of its nonphonetic nature, allowed people to communicate who could not have understood each other in a conversation. Latin had the same function in Renaissance Europe by being a written *lingua franca* (although unlike Pinyin it could also be used orally).

The most obvious conventions of written language are spelling and punctuation, and they were among the earliest to appear. In an alphabetic writing system, spelling is an attempt to represent the essential elements of the sound of a word, stripping it of its dialectical or individual pronunciations. As a convention of written language, spelling is among the hardest to change. Even if the pronunciation of the word has wandered far from the set of letters that represent it on a page, the written version tends to remain the same. In English, there have been many attempts to effect some sort of spelling reform, and they have all failed, in part because to effect such a change would mean recasting all the books in the British Museum and the Library of Congress, to mention but several million texts. There have been some changes over the course of time, but they are usually evolutionary or result from the development of a second version of the written language such as written American English, which differs in some spelling conventions from the British version. In most languages, however, spelling is relatively stable and became particularly so with the advent of printing, which tended to standardize written language across relatively large geographical areas and throughout entire languages.

Spelling is usually conventional within a language, but punctuation works its conventional way across languages. The period, the comma, the exclamation mark, and the question mark have become almost universal as marks, with little variation in their use or meaning. The meaning of the exclamation mark and the question mark, even when they are divorced from any text at all, is understood almost everywhere. They appear alone in comic strip balloons and on signs in all countries around the world. Other marks, such as the quotation mark, the colon, and the semicolon, are slightly less stable, but even these symbols are more or less constant across keyboards of typewriters and computers regardless of where those keyboards are. There may be extra letter keys and there may be different symbols for number and paragraph, but the basic marks of punctuation have become international conventional symbols and their meaning is stable. The differences that exist (such as whether single quotation marks take precedence over double ones, or whether periods, commas, and semicolons are placed within or without the quotation marks) appear to be national or regional conventions inspired more by the taste of some long-forgotten printer than by the necessity to establish a broadly applicable conventional symbol to indicate pauses, breaks, and changes in intonation.

If spelling and punctuation are the most obvious conventions of written language and exist primarily because it *is* written language, there are some conventions of grammar and syntax, however, that separate the written form of a language from its oral form. A few syntactic rules apply primarily to writing, and some have come to apply to language generally because of the influence of writing. To take an example of the first sort, in written English the following is ambiguous:

After taking a bath, the water was muddy.

The sentence makes "sense" only if you assume that people, not water, take baths. In oral language, the intonation pattern of both the introductory phrase and the main clause would make clear that the speaker had taken a bath and muddied the waters. There is no punctuation mark that can clarify the fact that the emphasis in the phrase is on "bath," so in written language the sentence is visually ambiguous and therefore "incorrect," and "After taking a bath" is a dangling modifier. It is harder to dangle modifiers when we talk (intonation clarifies the relationship) but easy when we write because of the visual proximity of words in writing and the lack of markers for certain intonation patterns. Thus, a particular syntactic convention has emerged for writing. A participle or other modifier is adjacent to what it modifies. If it gets too far away in space, one must rewrite the sentence to put the modifier in the correct position.

An example of a syntactic rule that results from the fact of written language but that has come to affect both written and oral forms is the rule concerning the double negative. In speech the first negative in a sentence like

He don't have no potatoes.

has passed out of hearing by the time the second negative comes along. The second acts as an intensifier or repetition of the first. But when the two are put down in writing they can be juxtaposed, and they therefore present the possibility of contradiction. The double negative in writing has come to be seen as a positive, and its meaning has extended to the oral form. So, even when we hear the example sentence, we can infer either that the man *has* potatoes or, more likely, that the speaker is ungrammatical.

Beyond grammar and syntax, written language has evolved a number of conventions that are peculiar to it. One is the paragraph, a unit of written discourse that has no clearly defined counterpart in oral language. It is usually defined as that which embraces a single large concept or event and its subsidiary concepts, illustrations, events, or characters. Such a definition is rather vague, as vague as the definition of a sentence. Although the sentence is a concept that derives intuitively from our uses of oral language, its various definitions include notions of "sentenceness" that are derived from written language. Many of what people would consider to be "sentence fragments" are so only in their written forms. Paragraphs are the pure creation of written language, however, and became stabilized as a form with the introduction of printing, where some sort of break in the text is necessary to please the eye of the reader and to free the reader from having to be extremely careful about where to fix attention. At first, paragraphs were close to being merely arbitrary breaks in the text; later the conventional definitions, most of which remain somewhat vague, were established.

So far I have been considering parts of a written text, those conventions that occur within texts of various sorts, but there are also conventions concerning the whole text—what has come to be known in literature as the *genre* (outside of literature, there is no similar concise term, although the term *text type* is frequently used). Oral forms of formal discourse such as the story, the ballad, or the epic, and, later, the oration developed conventions that signaled to the listener what was about to happen or what sort of discourse could be expected. So, too, did informal discourse. As various types of written discourse were formulated, they too developed and established norms and conventions with respect to length, opening, development or elaboration, and closing. The conventions applied to the content of the genre, or what it was appropriate to write about in that particular kind of writing, to how the writing should be organized, and to the particular forms of language that should be used.

By announcing that this volume is an essay, for example, I have triggered certain expectations in some readers and I have set certain constraints on myself. For example, I have announced that I am going to deal with content in such a fashion that a nonspecialist should be able to read and follow the text. I have announced that I will include speculation and conjecture as well as interpretation and analysis of the subject at hand. I have suggested an organization that is less rigid and formulaic than might be expected in a scholarly paper on the same topic, and I have announced that my tone will be relaxed and my language formal but not pedantic. I have also placed myself within a tradition that includes a number of people with whom I audaciously would have myself compared, from Francis Bacon to Lewis Thomas. All this I have done simply by selecting a genre with a known history and definition.

At this point in the history of the world, the number of genres and subgenres of written discourse have proliferated almost beyond the imagination. I explore the reason for this proliferation a bit more in the next section. One reason, however, is related to the specialization of knowledge that has occurred as knowledge has grown, as already briefly discussed in Chapter 1. Groups that wish to communicate with one another, but that do not see any particular advantage in having their communications make sense to a larger world, have developed their own genres with their own conventions. As a result, those in the academic world have special rules for writing scholarly reports in each of the disciplines and many of the subdisciplines as well. As I suggest in Chapter 4, these rules have an effect on how people in those disciplines "think." In the business world there are "house styles" for internal and external communications that are distinct for each company. The same is true of governmental organizations and social groups. Some of the differences among groups are relatively small, so that a typist can move from a job in one manufacturing corporation to a job in another with relative ease. If that typist were to move from a manufacturer to a hospital, however, there would be extensive new text types to learn, and the process of acclimatization would take several weeks at least.

Each of the genres, or text types, that has evolved has delimited what shall or shall not be included. In an American business letter, for example, it would be improper to include more than a cursory amount of personal information, and it would also be improper to discuss one's emotions at any great length. Such is proper in business letters written in countries such as China and Latin America. Similarly, in American scholarly writing in the sciences, the proper approach to the content is also to exclude the writer's personality. In the humanities, the word "I" is permitted. Documents also have conventions that imply that certain things have to be included, such as the business writer's address and the address of the recipient (even though that is on the envelope). The report of scientific research has to have certain things described, such as the treatment given in the experiment. Certain phrases and sentences are also obligatory to a genre, or text type; their absence may pass by the reader unnoticed, but they are significant and so would tell the alert reader that the writer is not fully acquainted with the rules of the game. An example would be "Sincerely yours" at the end of a letter or "The purpose of this [paper, study] is to" in the second paragraph of a scholarly paper.

As the genre, or text type, defines some of the rules as to the appropriate content of a piece of writing, so too it defines and is defined by how the material is organized. A story implies a temporal sequence, although not necessarily a linear sequence from beginning to end, for it can have flashbacks and other sorts of interruptions. In addition to the *temporal sequence*, there are three other major forms of organization. The *spatial* arranges the information according to a visual principle, as from left to right or top to bottom. It is also the organizational principle that permits a writer to put two things or ideas next to each other in order to compare and contrast them. In this respect, the text uses spatial arrangement as a metaphor, for it is arranged so that the reader may cross-reference the two items as if they were in tabular form.

The third and fourth types of organization are the *propositional* and the *appositional*. The first is based on a set of conventions about common ways of thinking. A writer establishes a point and proves it through one of a number of logical operations such as example, precedent, inductive reasoning, or deductive reasoning. Usually a propositional text makes a single point, or if it makes more than one, it announces the number of points it will make. This form of writing is one of the most frequent in business correspondence and in scholarly writing in most of the disciplines, except those that use temporal or spatial patterns of organization (for example, history or some of the natural sciences). Appositional organization does not assert a common logic; instead, the mind makes instantaneous connections, not all of which are completely logical. Appositional organization works by analogy and metaphor as well as by such devices as rhyme or even subconscious association of words and images. Appositional writing is often found in poetry, but it also occurs in much prose that is considered informal, such as a letter to a friend. It is also common in advertising and in ideological texts that appeal to the emotions as well as to the intellect. Politicians are particularly fond of appositional structures. In some cultures, appositional organization is considered appropriate even in formal and scholarly texts; it has become so for contemporary literary critics.

Together with the selection of content, then, the organizational principle provides a conventional definition of a genre, or text type. A novel announces that it will deal with people who are not necessarily real people and that it will apply a temporal principle of organization with beginning, development, and end. These become the expectations of a reader. A business letter announces that it will deal with matters pertaining to commerce, and the organization will be propositional. A dissertation in psychology announces that it will deal with matters related to human or animal behavior, that it will state its intention, review the prior research, describe the experimental or research design, including the various tests, present the results, and end with an interpretation of those results. When writers violate these expectations, they will either be rejected or hailed as innovators. The second is more likely for the novelist, for artists continually challenge and modify the traditions of convention.

The third defining point of a genre is the *style*, and the tone that is considered appropriate to that style. To take the examples from the preceding paragraph, the novel will use language that resembles speech but without some of the hesitations and pauses and repetitions that would occur in actual speech. The speech may be that of a highly educated person or a quite uneducated one, depending on the fictional character. The business letter will use a more formal language than the novel. It will avoid personal and intimate language, and it will strive to present the writer less as an individual than as a part of an organization. The dissertation will be even more impersonal than the business letter. The writer will not use the personal pronoun. There is no room for humor in the dissertation (a small joke is permissible in the business letter), and the writer must use language that is considered scientific and that contains the appropriate qualifiers and disclaimers that the writer has solved the riddle of the universe even if the writer feels sure that the solution lies in the dissertation if only the readers would admit it.

Written language, then, has evolved sets of conventions for the use of language ranging from the spelling of words up through the whole structure of a text that defines the genre of the text. Beyond that, it has developed a set of conventions that signal to the reader how the text is to be used in the world. When we pick up a novel, we expect to spend some time enjoying the experience of reading it. Ordinarily, we do not expect to get any specific information from it. Not so with the business letter, which is to be read for quite specific pieces of information. It also is primarily to be read by only one person, who is probably expected to write a reply to it. No one has to reply to the dissertation, but it is expected that others in the field will read it and include its name in their dissertations or reports of research in the same subfield of psychology. Each type of text, then, has a specific role. Some texts are counters in an exchange of texts. The writer of the business letter expects a reply to that letter from the addressee. If the writer sends a copy of the letter to several other people, whether in the writer's own organization or outside it, it is for their information only and they are not expected to reply to it. It is possible, however, that one or more of them will reply and send a copy to the others. Much writing occurs in a complex ballet of relationships among people. For example, when an American child receives a present from a distant relative, there is the expectation that the child will write a "thank-you" note to the relative. There is no obligation or expectation that the relative will continue the correspondence.

Much writing is sent out rather like the legendary note in a bottle from a desert island with the hope that someone will read the text and in some way act on it. Entire industries thrive on direct mail advertising with the expectation that about 2 percent of the recipients of the offer will respond to it. Other kinds of text are obligatory, such as the injunction attached to pillows and mattresses, "under penalty of law this tag not to be removed except by the consumer." Although one is not sure just who is expected to read the message and take it to heart, most people eventually do tear the message off despite being told that they will be imprisoned if they do so.

From the very beginning of written language, texts have seemingly been defined by conventions that set boundaries on what they will look like, how they will employ the symbol system that has been chosen, what content, organization and style they will have, and how they will be used in society. Written language necessarily is defined by convention, otherwise it could not do what was intended for it: transport information across time and space to oneself or to another person.

THE TRIBES OF SCRIBES

This point brings me to the fourth aspect of written language and text, one that has remained constant over history and geography. Writing is used in a social setting, which is to say that writing needs more than one person. There has to be a writer and a reader. Although there are still occasions when writing is entirely solitary, and people do have "private" languages and codes with which they write for themselves and no others, most of the uses of writing involve two or more people.

From what I have argued earlier, written language and texts mean that the two or more people must share knowledge. I elaborate on this point in Chapters 3 and 4, but set forth its basic nature here. The writer and the reader must agree on the visual layout and the significance of the way the information is stored and displayed. They must agree on the conventions of spelling, punctuation, grammar, syntax, and genre, as well as on how the text is to be used in the exchange of information between them. Finally, they must both know much of the information that is encoded in the text. Language is a symbol system; it refers to objects, events, ideas, and feelings. It does so in a somewhat elliptical but conventional form. When I write the word *text,* for example, I am using that word to refer to trillions of different sorts of texts from rune stones to aircraft maintenance manuals. I expect you to "read" that word and bring to mind, not the exact set of images that I have in my mind, but a close enough approximation. I do not need to provide the whole list. Similarly, when I read a recipe, I do so with some knowledge about cooking, ingredients, and the appearance and taste of food already in my mind.

The writing system is efficient because it is a conventional code that does not have to provide all the keys to unlock it every time a person sits down to write. The writer can assume that the reader will share a lot of information. This assumption appears always to have been held by writers and readers. The group of highly literate people in a society, those whom we call the scribes, have been distinguished by having in common a knowledge of the particular coding system that is written language. As we shall see in Chapter 4, this knowledge was and is complex; it is more than simply knowing how to sound out or make out the marks. Scribes were more than literate; they were learned. Having that knowledge set them apart from others, just as those who knew certain of the potions and spells that could alleviate pain were set apart by their knowledge. Extended writing appeared in society at that point where some sort of specialization of activities emerged. It is argued that writing really began to be a major factor in society with the emergence of the town as opposed to the village, just as the printing press became a useful adjunct to the rise of international commerce and capitalism, but was not a cause of the commercial change.

From the beginning of writing, then, the invention meant that its users shared a great deal of knowledge about the invention. The scribes in any society set about arriving at common definitions of the medium and its uses. Over the course of history, as new generations were inducted into the scribal society, they learned these definitions, but they also learned about the past of the scribal group. When written language began to embody religious, legal, and theoretical texts as well as commercial ones, many scribes also had to know the content of these documents in order to become part of the scribal society. Although in an oral culture, it was important for people to have common knowledge of ritual and custom, the scribal societies were able to accumulate more in the way of both text and commentary. They also began to decide which texts and which commentaries were most important to keep because the number of texts soon began to outstrip the number of scribes. Some of them were important, others less so. As in any society, the scribes began to decide what was integral to scribal culture and what was peripheral to it.

Scribal groups defined scribal culture and began to establish the rules for literacy. It soon became apparent that knowing the symbol system and the conventions of written language and text was not enough to be considered "really literate." I must distinguish here between the literate and the scribal. Many people during the course of the world's history have learned to read and write to a certain extent. In some societies, particularly some religious societies, such as Reformation Scandinavia or modern Islam, it was or still is necessary to demonstrate that one could "read" a segment of a religious text. In many cases, the individual memorized the test portion. This slight degree of "literacy" the people had enabled them to function within the society, but they were hardly masters of the written language in the way that scribes were. This distinction between the literate and the scribe has come to take on increasing social and even economic weight, and it looks as if the gap will only widen.

The scribe had to know how to read and write, had to know most of the conventions of written language, and had to know a body of texts, in part because the information contained in texts tended to be cumulative and to be self-referential. For example, I have chosen not to write an essay with hordes of footnotes or references in the text, yet I have, for example, mentioned other texts such as *The Iliad* and referred to people like Moses. I have done so with the assumption that you who are reading this text share with me knowledge of certain other texts so that we may use them as a kind of code within the code of written language.

Within our scribal culture, therefore, as within other scribal cultures of the past and of other languages and societies, there is an assumed body of texts the knowledge of which helps to define the members of that culture. In fact, it is this knowledge that many refer to as "culture." In a literate society, a person is cultured if that person has read the prescribed texts that are valued by the culture. *Cultural literacy,* as it is often called, is an important aspect of being a member of the scribal group, which is not the same as being a member of the larger polity.

I suggest that cultural literacy has been a part of being a member of a scribal culture for as long as there have been scribal cultures. I also argue that in any large scribal culture, such as that in the United States, there are

Texts often remain long after they have served their purpose. They can form a historical record of their own as we go from top to bottom reading the signs on this building.

also scribal subcultures that have their distinctive patterns of layout, their particular genres and other conventions related to reading and writing, and even their own set of texts necessary to being a full-fledged member of that culture. In order for you to judge my competence as author of this work, I should indicate to you that I have read some of the texts that mark members of the literary/linguistic scribal culture. I could do this with a chain of names interspersed in the text (which I have eschewed), with a bibliography (see the Afterword), or with a line

gelbongmcluhangoodywattmoffettderridabakhtinrosenblattjakobsonfoucaultsaid

and thus be done with the whole business of establishing my credentials.

That such scribal cultures exist is obvious; they exist in all fields and professions, and people are often members of various scribal subcultures. Each of these subcultures has its body of lore and its particular procedures for going about reading and writing, which are its primary means of inquiring into the nature of the subculture and reporting to other members of the subculture the results of the investigations. A simpler way of putting this is to say that to be considered a literate person in a company that deals in widgets, you have to know how to read and write like a widgeteer. You need to have the conventions of textual material concerning the making and selling of widgets; you have to know when to read and write what in the course of making and selling widgets; and you need to know some of the historical documents in the world of widgeting. Otherwise, you simply are not "in."

Keeping people out and letting people in is a part of every culture in the world, and scribal cultures are no different. They are quite exclusive. Because of the tremendous proliferation of information and texts, it is impossible for a person to read everything or to "take all knowledge as my province," as Sir Francis Bacon is said to have claimed. As knowledge has become subdivided, so have the scribal cultures. Even to be considered an "educated" member of a national culture, which is to say a national scribal culture, requires a minimum of twelve years, and then one is barely "in." To become a member of the scribal subculture of sociologists requires an additional eight years, much of which is spent learning to be literate in the specific terms of sociology. Besides reading the right people, one has to learn to read a sociology text as professional sociologists do and then to write a sociology report as professional sociologists do. Other things are involved as well, such as doing "field work," but the bulk of effort in learning to "be" anything in the literate world is spent in learning to be literate in the ways those who already are anything have defined literacy.

Although much has changed in the world of written language since that first mark on a stone or a clay slab, although complex machines have replaced simple tools, although whole industries have thrived and fallen during the course of making the means of reading and writing available, the fundamental nature of written language has remained constant. It is still a means of storing information in visible space according to a set of established conventions that gives the users something in common and thus sets them apart from other people.

CHAPTER 3

What Are You Looking at When You Read This and How Do You Know?
The Ontology of Texts

My claim in Chapter 2 that the appearance of writing made possible both the permanent storage of information and the sharing of that information may seem remarkably naive, given the current state of literary theory and even the philosophy of language and sign. In this chapter, I take up these various concerns and elaborate on them in the light of the constants about written language and its users observed in the first chapter.

To do this, I begin by stating the issue baldly: What does a text mean and how do you know? This issue has concerned various people who are called by such names as "post-structuralist," "reader response critic," "semiotician," "deconstructionist," and the like. I do not describe the various nuances of theory that divide various sects and partisans on this issue, but I try to sort through the issue and offer an explanation as to why they have arisen.

In Chapter 2, I wrote that written language is a system for recording information. The information is stored by human beings, who have an idea of what it is that is to be stored. It may be a list of things to be bought or sold. It may be a law. It may be the record of a bloody battle. It may be a story. It may be an observation concerning the workings of the universe. It may be the random or ordered ideas and images coursing through the writer's head. In each of these cases, the writer selects from the store of symbols used for written language a number of those symbols to represent the information that she wanted to store.

Once written, a text becomes disassociated from the writer. It stands on its own, or does it? How should we think of what we read? Is it true? What

An American text where different views produce different readings but cannot be read in a continuous way; as to its meaning . . .

does it represent? Are readers controlled by it, or do they have some say? How do texts relate to one another? Text can be seen as referring to something else. It can also be seen as a product of the writer's conception or perception of that something else. Now, when a reader comes to look at the text (let's say it is a reader who does not know the writer and cannot communicate with her), the reader has a problem. Can he be sure of what it was that she intended when she set the text down? Was it 4 bundles of bricks or 40? Was it that once upon a time there was a prince who had been turned into a toad or a prince who had been turned down by a toad?

I can represent this problem best by means of a diagram:

WORLD

WRITER   TEXT   READER

One writer creates a text based on her perception of the world. A particular reader looks at the text but has little else to go on in making connections between the text and the writer and her world. Of course, he can act as many readers do; look at the text and compare it with his view of the world and thus make judgments about the text and at times, by inference, about the writer.

In the history of people's thinking about the problems this diagram poses, there have been a number of ways of viewing them and coming to a solution of them. One can say that a text can be seen only as an object that is related to the world; the reader and writer are unimportant. A second view is to say that the text can be seen only in relation to the writer; intention is all. A third is to say that one can look at the text only in relation to oneself, the reader; the writer and the world are negligible compared to the reader's understanding. The final way is to say that a text can be seen only as something that is self-contained and that has little reference to writers, worlds, or readers; it is an object, related to other objects. Each of these positions has been advanced in the history of philosophy, and each is fallacious when taken as an extreme position (as are most extreme positions). I believe that one must assume that all texts involve a necessary compromise among positions and that the whole diagram must be seen as being brought into play with the consideration of each text that is produced or reproduced.

To some this issue may seem rather esoteric and of concern only to philosophers and literary critics. The problem of how to view texts, however, has its ramifications in the "real" world. It is a central issue in the field of law, for it raises the question of the meaning and interpretation of documents like the Constitution of the United States. It is the issue on which the confirmation of Supreme Court justices hinges. It is an issue when one considers how to treat contracts and the fine print on the back of sales and loan agreements. The question of the relation of the text to the writer, the reader, and the world also arises when one considers such issues as freedom of the press, censorship, and libel. If the text has meaning or value only in relation to the reader, then censorship and libel seem rather empty, although paradoxically it is the reader who imputes the negative value to the text even though the reader cannot admit that. If the text can be tied to the world, then censorship and libel take on very real meaning. What may seem to be rather abstract issues take on rather practical consequences.

I would also suggest that the position relating the text to the world was most vociferously held in those periods when there were relatively few texts as compared to the present time when the number of texts in the world probably matches the number of molecules of water in a good sized lake. The view that writing must be seen only in relation to the world comes primarily from persons who deal with religious texts. The view of writing as having its primary existence in relation to writers is also held by people who are primarily concerned with studying or thinking about how people create literary forms or who are concerned with providing rules for writers and with teaching the novice. As the number and variety of texts have increased so that people cannot possibly claim to have read anywhere near all of them, much less all copies of all of them, much less to know which is the final version of a text, perhaps the only way to consider the world of written discourse is in relation to the reader and what goes on in a particular reader's mind. One cannot generalize about texts and writers and the world.

An alternative way of viewing the plethora of texts is to say that the sea of printed paper can be examined only as a sea. Texts can be said to be related to other texts, but they cannot be said to have any real relationship to writers, readers, and the world, particularly if we cannot tell who wrote them or whether they represent any reality in the world or whether anybody ever reads them. The sea of stored information necessarily causes indeterminacy.

THE WORD IS THE THING

As I suggested in Chapter 2, written language developed as an information storage system in which actual objects such as bales of straw were represented by symbolic marks for them. The symbolic notations were arbitrary, but it was generally clear that a particular mark represented a particular sound, syllable, or object. If it represented an object, then it was a direct symbolization. If it represented a sound or a syllable, then it represented something that was itself a symbol of an object.

This basic feature of both written and oral language seems to have impelled people to think that there is some direct relationship between the symbol and what it represents. In the book of Genesis, Adam is said to have named the animals; many persons believe that these names somehow represent the true essence of the thing. Words are important because they are potent symbols. In many societies, to tell someone else one's real name was to give away something extremely precious, and the person who gave away this secret risked destruction. Such a belief is still prevalent in many societies; to name something is to have some sort of power over it. One of the first things people do with a new discovery such as a star, an element, or a moon of Uranus is to give it a name, even if it is a number. Such names mean that we know the thing. These early beliefs about the relationship between the name and the thing are deep psychological realities even today.

In addition to the psychological reality of words, and particularly names, the belief that written language can be seen as directly referring to an external world is what has enabled people to decipher writing that many had earlier considered unreadable or incomprehensible. It was not until the discovery of the Rosetta stone in 1799, for example, with its inscription in Greek and Egyptian (the latter in two versions, with hieroglyphic and demotic characters), that the first clue to understanding Egyptian hieroglyphics was found. The assumption on which Champollion, a French Egyptologist, undertook the deciphering held that the two languages and three versions probably said close to the same thing, so that the known language, Greek, could be used to help decipher the others. Similar premises helped to unravel cuneiform writing, the Mayan language, and the runes. Since written language refers to something, given an appropriate clue and a lot of hard work, one can assemble the elements referred to in relation to the text and thus find out about both. Knowing from other sources what the Sumerians traded, we can begin to unravel the symbol system they used for trading. It is now thought that some of the major mysteries, such as the Phaistos disk of Crete, may be undecipherable because they have no referent; they may be simply collections of symbols to be used by writers and therefore as meaningless as text as is a typewriter keyboard.

Another aspect of the view of text as directly relating to some reality comes from religious texts. In many cultures, the religious text presumably was transmitted from the deity through a prophet or oracle. The text or the utterance that preceded the text can only be seen as having a relationship to a higher reality than that we can see. It also takes on a particular immutability and authority that cannot be questioned. In some religions it is considered sacrilege to change the text or even to mark the text once it has been copied or printed. The book as object becomes sacred in itself. If it is sacred, then the words that it contains must refer to an external divine reality and have a particularly stable relationship to that reality if only we mortals could figure it out. At times, this view leads to fundamentalism in religion. At other times, it leads to the possibility of multiple interpretations and controversy, depending on how the obvious metaphor is read. The use of the word *day* in Genesis has led to a fundamentalist, literal interpretation and the subsequent tenet that the world was begun in 4096 B.C. The use of the phrase "inherit the earth" from the Sermon on the Mount lends itself to more than one interpretation. In context, it can be seen as being either literal or metaphoric, and if it is metaphoric, how the metaphor is to be understood becomes a point of debate.

If it is true that many nonliterary texts represent directly some reality, then one could argue, as did Aristotle, that the literary texts we know are fictions are nevertheless imitations of actions and therefore somehow related to the world. They may not be directly representational, but in another sense they are. The story of Oedipus is the imitation of a set of actions that are plausible (although perhaps somewhat improbable in terms of the ordinary world). They are plausible because they correspond to a psychological reality concerning the relations among people and their feelings and reactions to certain events and actions. The text imitates a world to which people can assent. Furthermore, when we read a story or a play, we talk about the people in that story or that play as if they were real, even though we know "it's only a story."

Thus it is that we can talk of a story's being realistic. The text, which is supposed to approximate our sense of the real world, is judged in terms of the closeness of the approximation. In the same way, nonfictional texts are judged by their "truthfulness," which is also an approximation of our sense of the world. At the same time, readers may separate "fact" in a text from "opinion." All these activities derive from a necessary belief that the words in the text do approximate something outside of the text. You probably judge the words you are reading now in part by the extent to which they approximate or match the understanding you have of the relation of those words to concepts in your mind or to things you can see or have seen. For people even to use written language, then, they have to assent in part to the idea that language and texts can be judged by something outside of themselves, that is, the world.

UNLOCKING THE WRITER'S SECRET

One might well say to the preceding paragraph, "Ah, that's very nice, yet isn't it true that language is a human construct, and therefore it is to be judged not in terms of its truth in relation to the world but its truth in relation to the writer's perception of the world?" This is to argue that although some texts may indeed be divinely inspired, most of them come from the hard work of scribes who have taught themselves to write. What you are reading is the product of a person named Alan Purves, and it must therefore be seen in terms of his view of the world; if you knew more about him, the book would be more understandable.

If one considers text primarily in its relation to the writer, one is arguing that the encoder of language is the only one who really knows the meaning of the code and that the writer's intended meaning is the goal of our understanding of a text. One is also saying that in writing, as in speaking or composing music or painting a picture, the individual creator is making one view of the world apparent. In this sense, the act of writing is always creative, for the text is an individual's personal interpretation of the universe, an interpretation that occurs even in the most mundane of contexts. A business letter, perhaps even a recipe or a laundry list, is an expression of the writer's view of the universe. It is less important that the names and marks on the laundry list can be verified by shirts and socks than it is that the writer has encoded information concerning an individual structuring of these objects.

It seems easy enough to grant the preceding, given that words are the loose things they are. Most speakers of English would agree that the word *cow* refers to a certain class of animals. At the same time, it is possible that no two people would have precisely the same definition or the same mental image of cows. It might even be that one user of the language would think of the term as including steers, bulls, and oxen, whereas another would consider it to refer to any female animal, and a third would restrict the meaning to domesticated animals that give a particular kind of milk and have such names as Guernseys, Holsteins, Jerseys, and Brown Swiss. Many students of language claim that no two users of language hold precisely the same meaning of the words they use. When one adds the meanings of all the words in an essay like this or in a novel or a play, then the nuances of the total that the writer has created might theoretically set that writer's view of the world far apart from that of any of the readers. One psychologist has suggested that we should distinguish between the *mind* of the word and the *meaning* of that word. The mind is the sum of all the images, emotional values, and understandings of a word within a person's head; the meaning is that aspect of the mind that is generally shared with others. The problem one has, even with this view, is that of determining which aspect of a word is properly its meaning.

One of the tasks of the reader is to divine the writer's intention or to get as close to it as possible. When we read a business letter concerning the price of milk when it is sold to wholesalers of a certain category, the nuances are trivial and it is relatively easy to divine the meaning. But what are we to make of a sign that says "No Smoking" in a room that is set aside for smokers? In a railroad car, the sign clearly means that the section of the car is reserved for those who promise not to smoke while they are in the section. Not so in this room, it seems . . . or does it? Is the sign urging people who do smoke to give it up? Is it making a snide comment concerning the smokers, or is it put up to show the meaninglessness of such warnings?

If such an ambiguity arises from a two-word sign, what about a law or a novel, particularly if it was written 200 years ago? Many critics and lawyers would say that we must try to approximate the intention of the writer. Such has been one argument concerning the United States Constitution. Critics and philosophers have attempted such approximation in many ways. The first way is to gather as many instances as possible of language as it was used by the author or the author's contemporaries. The assumption underlying this effort is that people are consistent in their use of words, that they tend to "mean" the same thing each time they use a word, particularly within the same text and within the same broad context of other words in a sentence or paragraph. Readers can, by a system of "triangulation" through a writer's other uses of the word in other contexts, determine rather closely what the word means in a particular context. It is conceivable, then, to determine with some degree of confidence what a writer such as William Wordsworth means by a word like *nature* in one particular poem. We can look at all the other instances of the word in his total output and from the "averaged" meanings in various contexts determine that the word in this instance does or does not approximate the average.

The procedure of seeking an average meaning of a particular writer's usage of a word is popular in literary criticism and in law, where one has to deal with words, particularly abstract words such as *equality*, and determine a consistent meaning for them, at the same time trying to make that consistency historical as well as contemporary. But there is doubt whether such a procedure can apply to the United States Constitution. We would like *equal* to mean today what it meant when the Fourteenth Amendment was passed. For a time it was thought that two groups of people could be separated in many ways but still be equal. We have now decided in the United States that such meaning is not what was intended by the framers of the amendment. If two groups are equal, they cannot be treated separately. But if that is so, can one create regulations that directly seek to make amends for the wrong done to the group that was badly treated? Is that not a misreading of the word *equal* as it was used in the middle of the 19th century by lawyers and philosophers of law and ethics in the United States? Such a consensual meaning, the intentionalist argues, can be derived and therefore can have authority concerning how readers should interpret a text.

Beyond determining the meaning of individual words, is there some way of deciding what the original intention of a writer was? One answer lies in the idea discussed in Chapter 2, the idea of convention. It is a convention of a particular type of discourse that it will contain certain kinds of information, be organized in a particular way, and have a particular style or tone. All these conventions help readers to interpret the meaning of the text, for they assume that the writer holds to the same conventional norms as most other writers. There are occasions when writers work to upset or destroy conventions, and then the readers often become quite upset and disconcerted. In most kinds of discourse, however, writers tend to stay within the conventional limits. In artistic writing, they often announce that they are modifying or violating the convention. A writer may say that the text is to be read as a "novel in verse" or a "prose poem." Another writer may change the normal expectation of appropriate content and write a tragedy about a traveling salesman. A third writer may include seeming nonsense words in a sonnet. Such announcements send signals to the readers that the conventional expectations are being challenged.

Another kind of convention about language and discourse lies in its uses. Human beings use language for specific purposes, such as to inform, to command, to inquire, to emote, to make pronouncements or judgments, and the like. A particular shape of sentence and paragraph has a particular force when used in discourse. A "No Smoking" sign is known to be an order, as is its visual counterpart, the red circle enclosing a diagonal line and a smoking cigarette. At times a sign is accompanied by a penalty assessment. The person who thought that the sign stating "Fine for Littering" was an invitation to dump the trash next to the sign clearly misunderstood the particular purpose implied by the sign and the word *Fine*. Signs of a particular shape and color with a particular form of text tell the readers of them what to do and what not to do. They are usually prohibitions, not invitations. The particular form of the sign, however, and its location and similarity to other signs with various injunctions and prohibitions indicate the intentional force of the message—a warning.

The intentional force (what philosophers have called the "illocutionary force") of texts is clearly a matter of convention and a compact among readers and writers that particular kinds of texts have particular purposes and therefore are to be read as having specific intentional forces. With a certainty—or near certainty—concerning the conventions of various kinds of text and their restrictions in the kind of information, the shape of the text, the style and tone of language and the intentional force, and with the assumption that writers use words consistently from text to text, readers often can get quite close to what it was the writer intended, particularly if they know something about the writer and how she used certain key words in other texts that she wrote.

IT MEANS WHAT I SAY IT MEANS

A careful critic of what I have written so far may well say, as have a number of recent theorists about texts and their meaning, "Yes, but we cannot really know what it was the author intended; it is all guesswork, and at times quite shaky. Why don't we just concentrate on what we get from the text?" These people would turn to the part of the triangle that concentrates on the relationship between the text and the reader. They reject the idea that there can be any objective view of the text's relation to the world and that there can be a real way of determining intention, which may in fact be irrelevant.

The fact that a piece of writing has been let loose on the world makes it fair game for any reader. An advertisement for shaving soap can come in the mail. We do not know who wrote it and do not care. It is there and we are to read it and on our own act on it and decide whether to buy the soap or not, or even whether to treat the text as if it were a poem and write a critical article about it. The reader can talk about the text, whether it was attractively set forth, whether it made sense, whether it was fun to read, or any one of a number of other responses to the text. The way a text is read is up to the reader.

But is the way one reads a text the same thing as the text's meaning? To a great extent, one would have to argue that the two are the same. If a person decides, for whatever reason, to read an advertisement as a poem, then legitimately the meaning of the words *advertisement* and *poem* becomes different. The reader has changed the intentional force from what most people would assume it is and has in effect rewritten the text and placed it in another genre, thus changing the meaning. We can see how this works in the two short pieces by Queneau (see pages 54 and 55).

Most people would agree that the writer of these two examples has taken the same information and by restructuring the text has somehow given it a different meaning. If a writer can do that, why cannot a reader? Isn't it a perfectly legitimate practice to assert that now one is reading a text as a person determined to find the Freudian significance of everything that is written? Or to read as a black or a woman? Each of these people is asserting that the stance we take toward a text changes the meaning of that text.

If this can happen as a conscious decision, does it not happen also unconsciously and inevitably? The world has changed since certain texts were written. There have been new discoveries and inventions, social shifts, and changes in the way in which we view language and the world. Many words in the various languages around the world have shifted in meaning, some almost becoming the opposite of what they originally meant. Most people today will see the word *lewd* in a sentence and not take it to mean "pertaining to the laity," which it meant several centuries ago. It would get them in trouble if they held to the original consensual meaning.

Just as words have changed in their meaning, so have entire texts. Some of the epic poems of the late 18th century, such as the *Columbiad*, now strike most readers as relatively silly. Such shifts can have important political ramifications. Many of today's readers, for example, see such works as *The Merchant of Venice* and *Huckleberry Finn* as racist; whether the works were racist initially is to them irrelevant. So, too, with works written at a time when the concept of women's rights was differently viewed. The views expressed by the school head in the children's book *Dimsie Goes to School* by Dorita Fairlie Bruce are now viewed as somewhat quaint or odd, whereas in 1920, when the book was published, they may indeed have been quite forward.

> "There are other things," went on Miss Yorke thoughtfully, her eyes on the flames, "that I am very keen to introduce here. After all, you're girls, and you'll grow in time into the women whom men marry, and on whom they will depend for the happiness of their homes. Oh, I know it isn't usual to talk like this even to the most senior of prefects, but this war has left our country, and our schools, too, very different from what they have been. Before the war girls learnt and played much as the boys. Games mattered above everything, and then, perhaps, study came next. Now, there is a third thing, which was always important, though very much overlooked, and to-day we can't overlook it any longer. Do you know what this is, Daphne?"
>
> Daphne's thoughtful grey eyes met the speaker's full, and a sudden flash of intelligence lit them.
>
> "Cooking," she replied with simple brevity.
>
> Miss Yorke gave way to an explosion of laughter.
>
> "I was going to give it a grander name," she answered. "I thought 'housecraft' would sound more attractive to the cultured ears of Jane's. Not only cooking, but sweeping and dusting, you know, and laundering. You are taught needlework already."
>
> "Yes," assented Daphne with a little sigh. "I know it's very sensible and necessary and all that, but," frankly, "the girls will simply hate it!"

Clearly the world changes, whereas texts tend to remain the same despite new printings; after all, that is why they were made texts in the first place. As people change, they view things differently. The text cannot, therefore, have a permanent meaning. It can be seen only in terms of the times of the people. We can make Shakespeare our contemporary more easily than we can become his. At least, that is what one group of critics asserts.

The implications of this view are many. One is that it is a futile attempt to determine what the original framers of a set of laws intended. We can never know, and besides, such knowledge is irrelevant. A law takes on a new meaning with each successive generation, not to mention the possibilities for it to mean different things to opposing groups in the same generation. In addition, a lawyer can use the body of successive interpretations of the law to justify the evolutionary rather than the static position of determining the meaning of a text. Thus, in the argument concerning the word *equal,* it is irrelevant to invoke intention in dismissing the idea of "separate but equal." Such an idea may have been an appropriate interpretation at the beginning of the 20th century. By the middle of the 20th century, society had changed in

Official letter

I beg to advise you of the following facts of which I happened to be the equally impartial and horrified witness.

Today, at roughly twelve noon, I was present on the platform of a bus which was proceeding up the rue de Courcelles in the direction of the Place Champerret. The aforementioned bus was fully laden—more than fully laden, I might even venture to say, since the conductor had accepted an overload of several candidates, without valid reason and actuated by an exaggerated kindness of heart which caused him to exceed the regulations and which, consequently, bordered on indulgence. At each stopping place the perambulations of the outgoing and incoming passengers did not fail to provoke a certain disturbance which incited one of these passengers to protest, though not without timidity. I should mention that he went and sat down as and when this eventuality became possible.

I will append to this short account this addendum: I had occasion to observe this passenger some time subsequently in the company of an individual whom I was unable to identify. The conversation which they were exchanging with some animation seemed to have a bearing on questions of an aesthetic nature.

In view of these circumstances, I would request you to be so kind, Sir, as to intimate to me the inference which I should draw from these facts and the attitude which you would then deem appropriate that I adopt in re the conduct of my subsequent mode of life.

Anticipating the favour of your reply, believe me to be, Sir, your very obedient servant at least.

"Official Letter" by Queneau. (From *Exercises in Style* by Raymond Queneau, translated by Barbara Wright. London: Gaberbocchus Press, 1958. Reprinted by permission.)

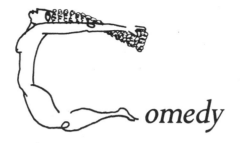
omedy

ACT ONE
SCENE 1
On the back platform of an S bus, one day, round about 12 noon.
THE CONDUCTOR: Fez pliz. (Some passengers hand him their fares.)

SCENE 2
(The bus stops)
THE CONDUCTOR: Let 'em off first. Any priorities? One priority! Full up. Dring dring dring.

ACT TWO
SCENE 1
(Same set.)
FIRST PASSENGER: (young, long neck, a plait round his hat) It seems, Sir, that you make a point of trading on my toes every time anyone goes by.
SECOND PASSENGER: (shrugs his shoulders)

SCENE 2
(A third passenger gets off)
FIRST PASSENGER: (to the audience) Whacko! a free seat! I'll get it before anyone else does. (He precipitates himself on to it and occupies it)

ACT THREE
SCENE 1
(The Cour de Rome)
A YOUNG DANDY: (to the first passenger, now a pedestrian) The opening of your overcoat is too wide. You ought to make it a bit narrower by having the top button raised.

SCENE 2
On the S bus, passing the Cour de Rome.
FOURTH PASSENGER: Huh, the chap who was in the bus with me earlier on and who was having a row with another chap. Odd encounter. I'll make it into a comedy in three acts and in prose.

"Comedy" by Queneau. (From *Exercises in Style* by Raymond Queneau, translated by Barbara Wright. London: Gaberbocchus Press, 1958. Reprinted by permission.)

such a fashion that "separate but equal" became both a logical contradiction and an anathema. The word *equal* was an absolute, like the word *straight*.

One of the objections to this approach to texts and their meaning is that it can lead to the idea that a text can mean whatever any individual reader wants it to mean. There is no possibility for a commonality among readers if each person's experience of words is unique. One recent answer to this charge can be stated in much the same terms that were set forth in the preceding paragraph. Texts do indeed have particular individual meanings and reverberations, but most people in a society share a portion of those meanings. There is an established community of readers who share the same ways of reading a particular text. This community is like the scribal communities. As a group, these people share meanings of words and texts. They share a way of reading, and for them the meaning of any particular text is a consensual one.

Such communities can be of various sizes and as communities can last various lengths of time. One community of readers may be small—for example, a sect that interprets a sacred text in a very particular way. An example is the Shakers, who have died out as a community. Other communities can be quite large, such as the relatively vast group of speakers of various languages who largely share the same interpretation of a tragedy like *Oedipus Rex*. That large community sets certain boundaries on its subgroups and the degree to which these can deviate from the general consensus. This shared international community is what is often meant when one speaks of the "Western heritage" or the "Western culture." It includes subdivisions of cultures such as the French and the American and even subdivisions of those groups. When I use the word *community*, I do not wish to imply that these are formless participatory democracies. On the contrary, they are usually hierarchical and authoritative, if not authoritarian, in the ways in which they would have their members read and interpret a text.

These communities share a common body of texts that are reference points, and they share common approaches to those texts, including ways of interpreting them and ways of talking about them. They have a common frame of reference that has been created by a group of scribal leaders. Some of these communities are large enough to be called cultures; some are smaller and are often thought of as schools. The important thing that cultures and schools have in common is an emphasis on the relationship between texts and readers. Readers make the text's meaning, but readers are also united by a common set of texts that are touchstones of what it means to be a reader in that particular culture or school. Having selected the texts that everyone must read in order to be considered a member of the group and then set the ways in which those texts must be interpreted, these schools have set the rules for membership in the group. The meaning is determined by the group of readers, not by the text and its relation to the world, nor by the writer.

THE TEXT AS A WAVE IN A SEA OF INK

One can object to each of these positions and say that they somehow miss the point. "We know that texts were written by people, even if we do not know who the people were. We know that these people probably had something in mind when they wrote the text. We also know that texts refer more often than not to something outside the writer, to some world of camels and straw or of geometry or fiction. We also know that different readers make different things of the text. But there is still a point that each of these positions and truisms misses. Each text, each piece of writing from a shopping list to a novel of Dostoevsky, has something in common with every other text since the world began." Some of these common points are discussed in Chapter 5.

But I could go further than that; I could attempt to be more rational about texts and treat them as scientists do atoms and electrons. When a person engages in this activity, that person begins to make certain assumptions about texts and writing: that they are points in a larger field as well as fields in and of themselves. In the first place, the scientific approach presupposes some sort of order and relationship among the various pieces of data. Even though the philosopher of science knows that the order is imposed on the data and is not inherent in it, there is still an assumption that the world is an orderly place. So, too, with the world of writing.

The first orderly assumption would have it that just as in spoken language there is a distinction between the norm of, for example, American English and each individual speaker's utterances of it, so too there is a distinction between something that I have been calling "text" and every individual instance of a text. The idea of a text is an abstraction but a necessary one. The next step is to see if one can determine the nature of this abstraction, so that its essential features determine what is a text and what is not a text. Some of those essential features are discussed in Chapter 2. A text contains information, it is displayed visually using symbols for language, and it employs conventions so that those who know the conventions can have access to the information. By this definition, a keyboard on a computer terminal is not a text because it does not contain information except for the information that the symbols displayed are those used by a certain group of writers. A radio broadcast or a performance of a play is not a text because it is not written down. There may be a text behind the performance, but the oral transmission is not a text. The following is not a text except to a cryptographer:

4rhypl wsqrn uuuos,, kl:p TWVCX.!1 u,frt- G

It uses symbols and conventions, but it does not use them conventionally.

Do we read these as text? Are they text or anti-text?

Each of these defining terms implies its opposite. The question then arises: Are there other structural characteristics of a text that will help us further define scientifically the idea of text? Notice that I use the word *structural*, a signal to some readers that I am engaging in what is familiarly known as *structuralism* and *post-structuralism*. I am trying to set forth rules by which anyone may, in fact, generate a text.

Some of the structures that have emerged during the course of this book are those that define what a written word is and what it is not; what a sentence is and what it is not; what certain figures of speech are— metaphors, for example. In addition, I have defined paragraphs and other segments of a text as well as whole genres, or kinds, of text. Again the principle of definition is to work in a binary fashion; one must define the metaphor, for example, in relation to that which is not metaphor, such as the description or the analogy or the simile.

Beyond defining texts through certain properties, people also define texts in terms of their uses. Any text should have some main function that one could ascribe to it. Probably the most complete definition of texts in terms of their functions in the world of human discourse is that of Roman Jakobson, who said that there were six primary functions of written (and oral) discourse. These can be seen in the following diagram:

Context

Message

Addresser--Addressee

Contact

Code

Both written and oral communications require a relationship between an addresser and an addressee. They also take place within a context (i.e., they are about something), and they contain a message that involves some sort of contact between the addresser and the addressee and that is encoded in language. Any message can emphasize any one of these six functions more than any other. As a result, the following functions of discourse can be identified depending on which one of the six is emphasized:

- *Addresser*: Expressive discourse emphasizing the writer's thoughts and feelings (a diary entry).
- *Context*: Referential discourse emphasizing the world outside writer and reader (an order form).
- *Message*: Poetic discourse emphasizing the expression itself (a poem).
- *Addressee*: Conative (or persuasive) discourse emphasizing the reader (a political message).

- *Contact*: Phatic discourse emphasizing the relation between writer and reader (a picture postcard).
- *Code*: Metalingual discourse emphasizing the language used to carry the message (a dictionary entry).

If the nature of text can be defined through some of its formal properties and conventions and also its functions as written discourse, cannot we also, many have asked, define the universe of texts through the information that is encoded? Thus, not only does the Babylonian bill of lading have something in common with a play by George Bernard Shaw in that both use language conventionally; they also have something in common in that when we read one of them we gain some knowledge of what is said in the other. Such would seem theoretically possible. Any one text can be said to draw on any other text not only for the way in which the symbols are arrayed but for what the symbols refer to. The principle behind this notion lies in the common-sense realization that after the first writer and reader, there had to be a necessary continuity in the spread of reading and writing through the people and through the texts that they produced. The connections between any two texts may be highly tenuous, but connections there are.

The idea of the connection of information within texts has its greatest appeal to critics who study literary texts and to legal scholars. One of the early assumptions of literary study was that writers of literature read the writers before them and so formed a long chain of influence that was either derivative or rebellious. There is some sort of historical progression from the first literary works to the very latest, if only one could figure it out. A particularly important aspect of this position is that which says that all writers of a particular national or ethnic group influence one another and that their texts have something in common other than the fact that they are written in the same language. This commonality of texts is what constitutes a national or ethnic literature, and particularly the "canon," or group of key interrelated texts in that national or ethnic literature, as well as the literature of those engaged in a field of study like physics.

Another way of viewing the connection among works of literature is through their specific forms or genres, such as the drama or the lyric poem. I have suggested this approach as marking one of the major structures that makes texts conventional. Each successive instance of writing in that form has an effect on the form and is related in both form and substance to each earlier instance. We can see that there is somehow a connection between *Oedipus Rex*, *Macbeth*, and *Death of a Salesman*. Each is a tragedy and each is a play. Each somehow has an implicit reference to the others and to all other tragedies and to all other plays.

Still another way of seeing the connection is to regard all the stories told as variations on a certain number of basic stories. This approach has a psychological appeal, particularly to those who see certain recurrent themes in dreams, myths, and legends. Texts, even texts from varying cultures, appear to have certain commonalities of content that deal with those very things that bind all human beings together: their biological, psychological, social, and religious needs and desires.

Some studies of folktales and myths, for example, suggest that these forms deal with a limited number of motifs, such as killing the monster or marrying the king's daughter. Others have suggested that all literature deals with a certain number of basic myths that are related to the seasons and harvest. All literature is thus interrelated through the way that it treats of humanity's deepest concerns.

The literary view of the continuity of texts is matched in law, particularly in those legal systems that have no single text as a constitution but that see each successive act as a part of a larger "text," which is the "constitution." All laws are interconnected and are cumulative. Such a view is also held in those legal systems that use court precedent. The idea is that each written opinion concerning a legal issue is part of a continuum of texts, so that although one decision may reverse another, it is necessary for the reversing justices to take note of the exception to the precedent. In doing so, the judges are acknowledging both the earlier views of text (that it must be seen in terms of the writers' intentions and in terms of the readers' interpretations), and they are adding to it a third view: All legal texts are part of a textual structure.

Viewing texts as comprising a larger structure does not necessarily address all the questions of meaning, but it suggests that if we view texts as autonomous but interrelated phenomena, they should not be related to the world or to writers, or perhaps even to readers. There is no standard outside the text, no authority by which we can determine what it means or whether it is truthful. We cannot ask of texts what they mean any more than we can ask it of atoms or molecules. We can ask how they work, how they are structured, how they are interrelated, but meaning is irrelevant because it is external to the text. All texts are about being texts. They may imply a writer and some readers, but they cannot be connected to any one person. This is particularly true in the age of the computer and the copying machine. People often have texts without authors, because they only have parts of them; they do not have definitive versions of texts, but drafts. In the scholarly world, for example, some of the most famous works of the philosopher Karl Popper were not actually published. The "writings" of Ludwig Wittgenstein and of the linguist Ferdinand de Saussure (who is often credited with being the father of modern linguistics and of structuralism) were not written by them. For example, Saussure's outstanding work on linguistics was posthumously edited and published from his students' lecture notes. Were they what the person wrote? Are they even Wittgenstein's or Saussure's words? There is no author in the sense of a writer, and so there is no *authority* to the historical figure reputed to have been the originator of the ideas—but perhaps not the words. So too with copiers and computers where we may have multiple versions of a text and cannot distinguish originals or authors. All are fragments.

In a sense, is not this the case of most texts? They are not the physical product of an author. They are produced somehow apart and through a complex human, mechanical, and electronic process. Did I write what you are reading? Perhaps, but what I wrote has been altered by many hands, from typists to editors to compositors. Can we really connect the text with a person? If we cannot, perhaps we should not connect it to a reader and certainly not to any world outside that of written language.

THE NECESSARY COMPROMISE

Each of these views of the triangle relating the text to the writer, to the world outside texts, to the reader, and to a solipsistic textual world has its intellectual appeal, and each has its proponents and detractors. Each is a part of the elephant as viewed by four blind men. The various views of text seem to neglect the essential nature of the compact by which we make and use written language.

Written texts function as a tool in the service of people and have become a part of the social fabric by which much of the world's affairs are conducted. They also serve as the records of people's thoughts, feelings, and imaginative speculations. In being all these things, texts are produced, read, duplicated, and circulated with the following assumptions, which are part of the compact to which the scribal world in all its manifestations has assented.

First, we operate on the assumption that any text has been produced by someone who had an intention or motive in producing that text. The text is not a set of random characters but is purposive in content, the organization of that content, and the choice of words and phrases. There may be multiple purposes—a writer may want to produce a text to earn money as well as to entertain a group of readers and inform them about her views of society. The point is that when we pick up a text we assume a rational force behind it, a mind that orders the world in language.

Beyond that, or contained within the first assumption, is the second assumption that the writer is using words according to a set of constraints or conventions that have been established over time within the scribal world of the writer and the reader. We assume, for example, that in the world of horticultural writing, the word *rose* refers to a particular genus of plants that share certain characteristics. Such an assumption is the semiotic compact that enables users of a language to communicate within limits. As I suggested in

Chapter 2, that compact extends to various visual aspects of text as well as to the characters and their groupings into words and sentences. The assumption of written language is that words have referents.

The third assumption is that since written texts exist in order to store and transmit information over space and time, they differ from the counters used in oral discourse when speaker and listener are together. The possibilities of misunderstanding are greater with written language because the reader is not there to ask what the writer's intention is, nor can the reader see the writer's expression. There are only the poor, naked words and symbols and the mind of the reader. The implication of these differences is that readers necessarily make meaning in a negotiation with the text rather than with the writer directly. Therefore, the reader does make meaning, in a way quite different from the way in which a listener understands a speaker.

In all that I have said, there is a final assumption that is a necessary aspect of the world of texts and literacy. According to this assumption, there is a necessary connection among texts, a connection that enables readers and writers to use the symbolic conventions. And the connection also enables them to consider the accumulation of texts and the information they contain as having an existence separate from, although related to, the people who make and read them. By its very nature, the world of written language has its own history and continuity both within a language, or writing system, and across systems. This continuity parallels those other human continuities that we see when we examine the human race socially, psychologically, and anthropologically. Each of these is a structure that we place on the human race, just as we place the theory of relativity on the spatio-temporal world.

Each of these assumptions concerning texts and the people who use them forms a part of the unwritten compact that the scribal society assents to and expects of its initiates. That I have written it down exposes the compact for readers and possibly makes it subject to revision. Another way of viewing this compact is to see it as involving three partners: a writer, a reader, and a text. The writer and the reader never deal with each other directly. The writer deals with the text in setting forth ideas, feelings, and images. The reader also deals with the text in evoking the ideas, feelings, and images from it. The text also deals with the world of things, events, people, and other texts, and it is because of this dealing that we can have continuity among writers and readers. We can see each of these dealings as a transaction in that the person and the text modify or are affected by each other. Similarly, the individual text modifies and is modified by the world of texts and the world outside of texts. I explore this set of transactions in Chapter 4.

CHAPTER 4

What Scribes Do All Day
The Psychology of Literacy

Having examined something of the origin and nature of literacy and the ontological issues that written language has brought with it, I now consider how people act when they engage in the activities of reading and writing. The reason for this exploration is that to many psychologists these activities appear to provide the closest glimpse into the mind itself. When people use language, and particularly when they use written language, either producing it or receiving it, they use their ability to think and reason. When people write and read, their emotions are brought into play as well; I do not wish to imply by using the word *reason* a divorce between the rational and the irrational.

I want to make two other caveats at the beginning. The first is that I do not use the currently fashionable word *process*, but *activity*. The reason is that I find the word *process* to be overused and to have various connotations that do not apply to reading and writing. People tend to see processes as being somehow mechanical and involuntary, particularly within the human body. Processes also have the unfortunate political overtone of being curiously unending and a substitute for the thing itself. Thus, we need not have peace, only the "peace process," whatever that is. Finally, the word suggests some of the worst aspects of the manufacture of food products. Is a poem really of the same order as processed cheese spread? I think that the term *activity* is more congenial for describing what goes on when people read and write.

The idea of activity comes from Soviet psychology (and particularly from the followers of Lev Vygotsky) and is used to describe that which an individual engages in with some purpose or end in mind. The end of an activity is to effect some sort of change in oneself or on the environment. It does not exist for its own sake. That seems to be true most of the time when people read and write. They read something for some purpose, if only to keep from being bored. They also write to effect some change; they will occasionally "doodle," but to most of us "doodling" is not writing. An activity is, then, something people consciously choose to do. It consists of subordinate acts and operations, so that any activity is necessarily complex.

The second decision I have made is to consider reading and writing as separate but complementary activities. Some psychologists and educators have been suggesting that reading and writing are the same. They do have one crucial point in common: The reader and the writer share an immense amount of knowledge about the world and about written language. At the same time, some fundamental differences separate writing from reading. In the first place, the purpose for writing something is usually quite distinct from the purpose for reading something. We write in order to record information; we read in order to retrieve information. As was suggested in Chapter 3, there are a limited number of functions of discourse, but the reader and the writer may not have the same function in mind with respect to a given text. The writer may want to persuade the reader to do something, but that does not mean that the reader picks up the text with the intention of being persuaded. Not only are the activities distinct in their general intentions; they are also distinct in certain of their individual acts and operations.

Nonetheless, in the rest of this chapter, I consider reading and writing simultaneously. I begin with the point of commonality between the two: that both the reader and the writer share many kinds of knowledge. They share all the kinds of knowledge about the conventions of text and the scribal world that they inhabit. This large burden of shared knowledge is clearly crucial if the writer and the reader are to share a text and the information in it. Then I consider some of the crucial distinctions between the inscribing of a text and the skills of decoding it that writers and readers must have. Finally, I consider the meaning-making acts that they must bring to bear when they enter into their separate transactions with a text.

The separate transactions that accomplish meaning-making were discussed in the preceding chapter. The reader and writer, I suggested, make a practical compromise when they enter into the world of literate behavior. They agree on the writer's having an intention (which may be ascertained through the text), on the words being related to some sort of reality outside the text and at the same time being related to the world of texts, and they agree that the reader has the capacity to get his own message regardless of what the writer may have had in her mind. With this compact in mind, then, both the writer and the reader begin a *transaction* with the text. It is not a transaction with each other, because neither is sure who the other might be and one cannot have a transaction with the unknown. The transaction is between the mind of the writer and the page or the screen. After that transaction is completed and the text is freed from the writer, then a new transaction between the text and the reader takes place. Each of these two transactions involves both a mental image of the text (what I call the model, or the meaning, of the text) and the text itself.

One could make an analogy here between literate activities and music. A composer usually has a set of tones or sounds in mind; she hears in her mind's ear a symphony or a sonata. This she sets down as marks on a page. These marks do not become music until they are played, that is, "read." Professional musicians, especially conductors, can look at the marks and "hear" a symphony, but most of the time it must be translated by musicians. With a written text that uses words, not notes, the reader may say the words aloud in the course of making meaning, but most experienced readers read silently, so that they do indeed "hear" the poem or the story mentally without requiring an oral interpreter. The distinction between the musical score and the text is less important than the analogy. In both cases, the text/ score acts as an imperfect bridge between two distinct transactions.

As was also suggested in the preceding chapter, there are two additional transactions in the world of text. Texts, using words as they do, refer to some extent to that which lies outside of them. They are imperfect representations or symbols of that outside world. Any noun fails to capture all the aspects of what it refers to, yet at the same time by being encapsulated in a word, the phenomenal world is modified for us by that bit of definition, just as the world modifies the word. There is, then, a transaction between the two. Similarly, there is a transaction between the individual text and the text type, or genre, of which it is a specimen. Again, there is a mutual modification.

All these sorts of transaction occur in the production and reception of any text. It is the nature of this activity of making transactions that we explore.

Although I find the psychology of reading and writing an interesting matter for contemplation and exploration, I am not convinced that such study unlocks the workings of the mind in general. Being a scribe is not the same as being sentient. My reason for suggesting a more modest approach to this aspect of literacy comes from what I said in Chapter 2. What the mind does when encoding or decoding a text depends to a certain extent on some of the inevitable features of written language and text. The text is there as an object in space. Readers and writers operate in time but in time relative to that spatial and unchanging object. This means that readers and writers can go back to the text again and again. What this implies for the writer is of incalculable value. The writer may change the text, and even add or take away large or small portions of it. The reader may also go back to portions of the text or may skip over portions. This aspect of text and its relation to reading and writing is strikingly different from speaking and listening. Only with recording machines and now videotapes can we go back and forth to recapture oral language. One can change and edit these tapes and records, but one cannot, for example, change or edit or go back over a conversation. Once said and heard, the utterance is irretrievable and unalterable. You can't "take back" what you have said, and another person cannot un-hear it. Paradoxically, there is a metaphysical concreteness or objectivity to oral language and a mutability to written language. These characteristics coexist with the fact that sound waves are gone quickly and texts can remain in libraries for years and centuries with little or no change. Conversations always take place in the here and now. One does not always hold back what one wants to say, nor can one "take it back." Writers can always hold back their texts and destroy them.

COMMON KNOWLEDGE
IN THE SCRIBAL WORLD

Chapters 2 and 3 discussed some of the knowledge that is required of a scribe. I review it here because it is important to correct the impression that scribal writing and reading are skills. The implication of this false impression is that somehow writing and reading are really quite simple once one has mastered the basic techniques, just as cross-country skiing is simple once one has learned how to stay upright and not to cross one's skis. Being scribal, however, particularly in the complex world of information that we inhabit, involves a great deal of knowledge that, as much as we have acquired, ever lies before us to be acquired. Let me simply list the items that a scribe knows:

1. A portion of information that is to be encoded or decoded.
2. The graphic symbols for encoding that information.
3. The techniques for encoding, given the available technology.
4. The graphic symbols for structuring information into a text and the graphic symbols and graphic structures appropriate to various genres, or text types, within a given community.
5. The genres, or text types, that are conventionally used for storing particular sorts of information, including the selection of information, the structuring principle for that information, and the styles and tones of language appropriate within a community for that genre, or text type.
6. Something of the history of those genres, or text types, including classic examples as defined by the community.
7. The conventions about ways particular texts and text types are used in various situations.

8. The relative importance of various texts and text types in a community.

9. The appropriate ways to approach various texts and text types in a community.

I will comment on and gloss a few of the particular items that readers and writers must know. I wish to impress on you the tremendous amount of knowledge that you bring into play when you read this volume. Those items include knowledge of the means of text production, which is clearly important knowledge for many people. To write this book, as I have, on a word processor requires knowledge of certain things our fingers have to do to make the text appear and remain in the memory of the computer. I do not know nor must I know much about computers, but I do know something about the various facets of book production so that I can seek to make this text available to you. This knowledge parallels the knowledge of a child using a crayon or pencil, or that of a stonecarver who makes monumental texts in graveyards, or of a Chinese brushpainter and calligrapher. It is clearly highly important knowledge, for without it information storage and transfer could not take place. The literate person in a scribal community has a rudimentary working knowledge of the operations of the literacy industry itself and of its operations in that community.

I should reiterate a point that I made at the beginning of this chapter. When I use the word *knowledge,* I do so with the full realization that toward everything that people "know," they have an attitude or a feeling. Knowledge is never coldly undertaken. When people say that they know a particular word or know the meaning of that word, they also have some set of feelings toward the image or the concept that the word embodies. So it is with genres, or types, of text. People look at a short story or a business letter with a set of predisposed feelings toward the form, as well as toward the content, the language, and the author or the person to whom or for whom the story or letter is written. Because writing and reading and texts occur in a social sphere, emotional as well as rational thought is always brought into play.

To return to the list of nine items that a scribe knows, it is clear that if a writer is to store information, she must have the information available to her in order to store it. Some of the information may be in her head; other information may be in books or in objects she sees or hears or touches or tastes or smells. All this seems relatively obvious, but what about the reader? After all, we read to get information, don't we? Yes and no. To read this essay you must know the meaning of about 80 percent of the words in it. You may have begun this book without much knowledge of literacy and its history, but you must know what the words mean as you progress through the text. I can give you a new word in the first paragraph and explain it to you, then you know it—or so scholars think. They can use that word expecting you to have turned the information into knowledge. I could not plunge you into a complex world of biochemistry without a series of introductory steps, nor could you read a text in that field without already knowing a great deal about what was going to be in the text.

As is also clear, people have to be able to visualize the information they know. They must know the symbol system and how the symbol system relates to words. In some languages this is more complex than in others. Some alphabetic languages, like Finnish, are to a large extent phonetic, at least for the dominant dialect. English orthography, on the contrary, is no longer anything near phonetic, so that learning the appropriate written symbols for words is a problem even for most English-speaking people and a serious one for the person learning English. Learning the symbol system of a nonalphabetic language is, obviously, quite a complex operation. In some languages, only a few people know all the symbols, just as in other languages, only a few even approach knowing all the words.

Clearly, knowing the meanings of words and knowing their spelling and visual encoding are necessary steps in both reading and writing. As suggested in Chapter 2, however, there is more to reading and writing than simply knowing the words and their symbols. The graphic world that has developed in the past 4,000 to 5,000 years has resulted in a tradition of ways of presenting text that it is necessary for readers and writers to know. Punctuation marks, white space around words, letter size, type face, the use of headings, diagrams, figures, tables, and other graphic conventions are part of the working knowledge of most writers and readers. This knowledge can be quite general (the sequence of pages and the visual format of paragraphs), or it can be quite specialized (maps, flow charts, and wiring diagrams, each of which has its elaborate conventional symbol system).

In a text-rich society, these visual symbols are elaborate in their significance. One can look at parts of a newspaper, for example, and tell which parts contain news and which advertising. Without knowing the language, a person knowing the visual conventions of newspapers can locate the television section or the classified advertisements. Returning from a brief trip, a person can sort through the accumulated mail and tell from the physical appearance alone which envelopes contain bills, advertisements, business correspondence of importance, or personal correspondence, although one can often be misled by the physical appearance of an envelope into assuming that what is actually a solicitation is a business letter.

A set of visual conventions is quite complex, and in more specialized scribal groups, judgments are made about writers on the basis of their use of space regardless of what information fills it. Teachers usually have a good idea about how much students should write in response to certain assignments, and they may make what seem to be hasty (but later prove to be accurate) judgments on this basis. Persons who want to sell a product know that they have to devote a certain proportion of the text space to the positive features of their product and a lesser amount to the negative features of their competitors' product. Scholars in a given field know by the placement of the text where to find the salient parts of an article in that field.

A part of the knowledge of the graphics of text is related to the knowledge of genres and text types. Various kinds of texts have visual conventions, but they also have conventions about the inclusion or exclusion of information, the placement or ordering of that information, the kind of language that is appropriate, and the tone of "address" to be used in presenting that information. The person who is writing a recipe is allowed to be chatty and

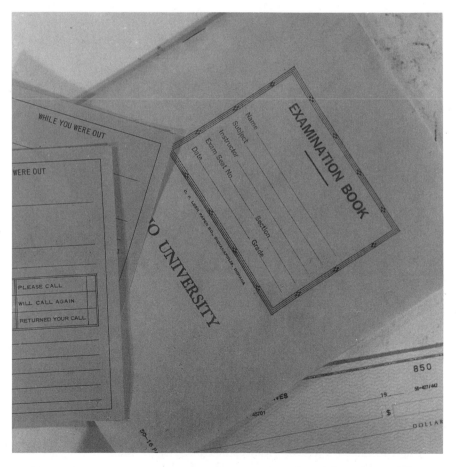

These text types provide their own environment and cue the writer and the reader.

familiar in the introduction of the dish and in comments after presenting the recipe. But the actual listing of ingredients and the sequence of preparation, and even the language in which these are presented, are rigidly prescribed. One cannot be vague, for the reader expects a certain amount of precision that allows him to reproduce the dish exactly. In the days before writing, one cook taught another by visual demonstration, in which showing a handful was sufficient because the novice could see the hand. In printed recipes the measures must be standardized and a "handful" must become a number of cups, teaspoons, or tablespoons. Some fillers or seasonings can be listed in terms of dashes and pinches or "to taste" because these are permissible variations that will not have a major effect on the dish.

As already mentioned, any genre, or text type, is defined by its conventions of content, organization, style, and layout. Some genres, however, are more rigid than others in the degree to which they allow variation from the convention, and the writer and reader know the limits of tolerance for each. People who make dictionaries and other reference works have much tighter standards than do the people who make novels or journal articles for a popular audience. Some industries and businesses have elaborate "house styles," and the publishers in certain fields have extensive style manuals to help the novice or even the expert writer. Most of these rules are made explicit for the writer, but they are implicit for the reader, who will be aware only if they are violated, which will disturb his reading of the text. Many of these rules and conventions have been established to produce consistency across writers, particularly when the works of several authors will appear in the same volume.

For many types of text, or genres, the writer has less worry about conforming to a set of rules and restrictions. As I said, I chose the genre of the essay because it allowed me greater freedom than would have the genre of the article or the scholarly volume. The novelist has a greater amount of freedom than I do, although there are restrictions placed on the novel by the marketplace. A person who wants to sell a "historical romance" has to conform to more conventions of content, organization, and style than does a person who is writing an "experimental novel" and does not depend on sales for her livelihood.

In addition to knowing the conventions of various genres and text types, writers and readers must have knowledge of some of the significant texts that have been produced within any particular genre. In a sense, one could argue that to know the one is to know the other. One learns the conventions of the genre through reading examples of it. It is possible, however, to read a book on the art of writing business letters or the art of writing plays and not have read any examples save the ones in the book—and those may be excerpts and not whole letters or plays. By not knowing those examples, the writer or the reader is somewhat like the person who has read all there is to read about sailing 12-meter yachts and has stayed on dry land the whole time. The experience is vicarious, not virtual, and vicarious experience does not fully prepare us for the rough and tumble of the real thing.

There is another aspect to the importance of knowledge of examples of the genre. As I wrote in the previous chapter, the structuralist position would have it that texts refer to one another, particularly texts in the literary genres, but also texts in law, history, and most of the academic disciplines. To a certain extent, texts also refer to one another in business, journalism, and even advertising. Certain advertisements rely on the reader's knowledge of other advertisements. The text plays against other examples in the type. As previously stated, in a particular culture or subculture, this knowledge is often referred to as cultural knowledge, or cultural literacy. It is an important kind of knowledge in both oral and literate cultures, but in a scribal world, knowledge of the classical texts of the particular scribal culture is what marks the full member of the culture from the neophyte.

Texts make transactions with other texts in a number of ways. At times, there might be direct allusion and commentary. A review of a book refers to the book. The reader of the review need not have read the book but should have some knowledge of the subject of the book. The critical discussion of that same book will presuppose that the reader has read the book but is not perhaps as much of an expert as the writer of the book is. As a result of this difference, the review will probably be more explicit although less detailed about the content of the book than will be the critical article. In philosophical and other disputatious texts, there may be some quotation from the opponent, but in many cases, the writer will assume that her readers have read many of the same "major" texts. At times she will be somewhat malicious and "pretend" to assume that the reader has read some obscure text that she is sure he has not.

Other kinds of texts, such as novels or poems, often use implicit allusions, a word or a phrase that makes reference to an earlier text and so uses that earlier text and what it contains as a symbol for an entire series of concepts. Thus we can refer to someone as a Romeo or as having the patience of Job. Again, we assume a certain amount of familiarity. At times the allusion may not be to a name but to a similarity of plot or situation. Even a phrase or sentence may be quoted. When William Faulkner wrote "The Bear," he used the last two lines from John Keats's "Ode on a Grecian Urn." The character discusses the lines, but Faulkner seems to assume that the reader knows the whole poem and perhaps even something of the situation of John Keats. The two lines evoke a whole textual world. (Just so have I alluded to both Faulkner's story and Keats's poem on the assumption that you have read both of them, or if you have not read them, that you at least have a familiarity with a parallel example.) At times this sort of evocation is crucial to the text; at other times it serves as a sort of literary caviar and caveat.

I cannot emphasize enough the centrality of this kind of knowledge in certain scribal societies. It is an important aspect of literate nationalism. As colonized societies looked forward to their independence or began their struggle for that independence, many of their leaders saw that one of the most important ways to establish the new nation was to create a national literature. Some of those leaders deliberately set out to form a national literature and to cut it loose linguistically and textually from the literature of the colonizers. This was the case in Indonesia in the 1920s. Cultural knowledge and a canon of texts are also a part of the identity of various groups within a society—for example, literate blacks, feminists, and intellectuals of various stripes and spots. It is not enough to hold the concepts and the conventions of the group; one must also know certain of the exemplary texts. Many groups have the problem of determining which texts are the most important ones and how thorough a knowledge of them is a prerequisite for full membership in the society.

The last three sorts of knowledge that I listed—of conventions, genres, and specific texts—comprise what can be referred to as the ritual nature of a scribal society. In a world of texts, where written language confronts one from the moment one's eyes open in the morning until one closes them at night, the individual would be lost were it not for knowing how these various texts are to be used. Imagine living in the United States believing that you are obligated to a respond to every piece of mail you receive! It would occupy most of your time; it would bring a surplus to the United States Postal Service; but it would surprise the sender of a direct mail catalogue to receive a letter thanking her for a nice catalogue, even though you had decided you didn't want anything this month.

Various groups and subgroups in the scribal society have devised rules for determining on what occasions one should write what kind of text, what those kinds of text are used for, and how they should be read. These rules are quite elaborate, and the more texts an individual has to work through during the course of a day, the more elaborate those rules become. In some workplaces, there are individuals whose only job is to screen texts for others. Those who do it for themselves make decisions continuously depending on their knowledge of the textual world that surrounds them. They read the morning paper, but not the cereal box (unless the paper has not arrived); they do not read the labels on their automobile as they go to work but do read the gas gauge. On their drive there are some signs that they read with care, and others that they know have little effect on their lives. As they sort through the mail, they may note those letters that deserve immediate response and even know what sort of language to use in responding to them. In the academic world, we can respond informally and tersely to an invitation from a colleague to attend a meeting. We must use formal language and make sure the format is correct when we are writing a letter of recommendation for a student. We know that certain notices of meetings are for our interest only;

others are commands. We have a sense of the intentional force of many of the documents that appear to the outsider to be worded in a similar fashion. The cues for this sense that we have may come from various peripheral aspects of the text such as the way the address is written, the kind of paper, and even the kind of typing or printing.

Within a particular field or discipline, its members soon learn some of the appropriate behaviors that mark them off as scribes in that field. I have noticed that when students begin at the university, they assume that each of their textbooks is to be read the same way. The reader is to mark the salient point of the text by underlining it or using a bright marker. Such a technique may work in texts which are highly redundant, but some texts, particularly in mathematics and the sciences, have little redundancy, so that the appropriate marking behavior is to draw pictures or work out the problems in the margin. Students also soon learn that a long reading assignment in history is about 150 pages; in mathematics it may be four pages. Yet an equal amount of time is needed for each.

Each of the decisions that people make both as readers and writers during the course of a day is based on knowledge of the textual world of the particular subgroups of scribal society that they inhabit. Clearly, this knowledge is as much a part of being literate as is knowing the alphabet or the works of Shakespeare. I argue that knowledge concerning how texts are constructed, understood, and used in our society is as complex a form of knowledge as that embodied in many a textbook on an abstruse subject.

HOLDING THE CHISEL
AND READING THE RUNES

Readers and writers share an immense amount of knowledge that they have accumulated over the course of lifetimes, and it is knowledge that is built on the lore of earlier generations. People who read and write need to translate that knowledge into text or translate text back into knowledge. In many cases, people seem to learn these two activities simultaneously. For sighted people, reading and writing obviously involve the eye, but the writer must also usually use her hands. The dexterity of the writer clearly is involved with the materials that the writer has to use. Probably the skywriter has to employ the greatest amount of skill in using the medium; much more is involved than simply shaping the letters. A person operating a word processor has a much easier time of it. Clearly, the medium that one chooses to write in and the surface on which one chooses to write affect the dexterity and other skills required of the writer. In some cases it may take a great deal of time to learn to enscribe text; for certain calligraphers and stone masons, the apprenticeship may take years.

Shoe cartoon. (From *Shoe*, November 19, 1985. Tribune Media Services. Reprinted by permission.)

Regardless of the medium, the writer must develop the ability to produce legible and even attractive text. The physical representation of the words and the ideas they express should be such as to enhance them, not to make them obscure. In some cases the desired effect is to make the physical appearance of the text unnoticeable; in other cases, the text is to be viewed in and for itself. People who make the frontispieces of art books or who cut monuments clearly want to be known for the beauty of their work. Newspaper compositors probably care not at all; theirs is a text that will be read and forgotten or used to wrap the fish. There is no need for the eye to be distracted by the shape and form of the letters.

Inscribing text requires more than manual dexterity and the creation of a visually readable if not beautiful text. It also means using knowledge about written language and its semantics, spelling, grammar, and punctuation. For a reader to consider the content of a written text, the writer must make sure that she has not created a text that is distracting in that it calls attention to its superficial characteristics rather than to the ideas. For many student writers, these concerns are paramount. They are equally important in the workplace and in the leisure-time use of literacy. Readers generally expect that they will not be distracted from the message by imperfections in the medium. Therefore, they notice typographical errors, spelling errors, poor handwriting, sloppy margins, and ungrammatical prose. The reader will often make a comment about the intelligence or the care of the writer or compositor. In today's world of computer-assisted text production, most of the errors that creep into text result from the faulty intelligence of the electronic proofreader.

In a recent newspaper article appeared the phrase, "If things do not improve our protests will emasculate to violence." Clearly the computer's text-editing program could not tell that the word was wrong; such programs can detect only a nonword. The error is noticeable to many readers because it detracts from the message of the text. Such an error in a newspaper article, which most people expect to read in a particular way, is especially noticeable.

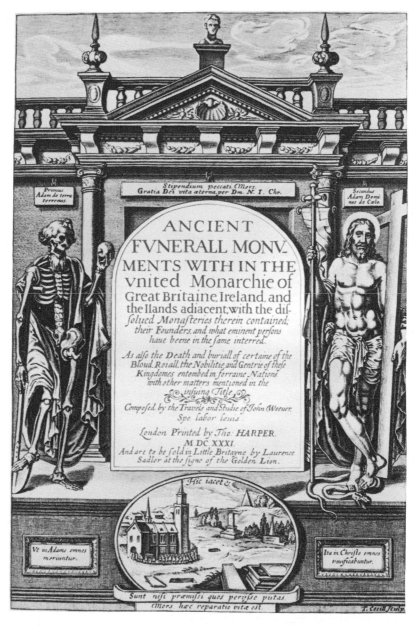

The title page of John Weever's *Ancient Funerall Monuments* (London, 1631) is a good example of typography that calls attention to itself as art. (From *Visible Words: A study of Inscription in and as Books and Works* by John Sparrow. Cambridge University Press, 1969. Reprinted by permission.)

As we see in the next section, if the error appeared in a poem or a short story, it would also be noticeable, but we would assume that its use was deliberate, not erroneous, and would seek to incorporate the word into a web of esthetic meaning.

The writer has to learn all these mechanical and enscribing skills, but readers have an easier time of it. The reader's main job in decoding the text is using the eye and turning the page. A number of skills are needed to become adept at reading, but they do not change according to the medium in which the text is presented, as do the skills needed by writer. The major skill in reading is that of matching the visual symbol either to an aural symbol or to an idea or image. In some languages this task is easier than in others, as suggested earlier. Where it is more complex, the reader learns such other tricks as using the context of words to decipher an individual word.

In addition to "cracking the code," most of the procedures for reading are learned quite effortlessly by the majority of scribes around the world. The major text-deciphering tasks that readers must employ involve modifying the amount of time taken to decipher a particular text. When people have to read a great deal, they develop speed and the ability to scan a page for the salient word or phrase. They are able to do this because of the redundancy of most written texts (as well as most oral discourse). This redundancy is built into the language to allow the information to be caught on the fly in conversation or speech, and the same feature has become a part of most texts. Only those advertisements for which one pays by the word or those writing contests in which the message must be "in twenty-five words or less, neatness and accuracy count" does the writer have to forgo the redundancy usual to most written language. As with other aspects of written language, the writer must learn to be appropriately redundant, to use words and other linguistic devices to connect sentences and ideas. This controlled redundancy in written texts is called *cohesion*, which includes a variety of devices to make the connections among phrases and clauses evident. The reader makes a much less conscious effort to note the various cohesive ties between sentences and clauses and, in fact, may only notice them by their absence. As the reader becomes increasingly facile, he is able to use such items as paragraph breaks and the knowledge that the salient information is usually at the beginning or the end of the paragraph to speed up the search for the appropriate information.

Much of the skill in the deciphering aspect of reading is skill in locating information, a skill that is clearly based on the knowledge of the conventions of text types and graphic layouts appropriate to different types of text. Once one has the system of the telephone directory in one's head, one can increase speed in finding a particular name. Almost instinctively, the telephone book reader uses alphabetic knowledge as well as some knowledge about the frequency of surnames that begin with different letters in order to locate the approximate page of a particular name. A quick turn of more than one page will get the reader closer, and then a fairly fast scan of the columns will bring one to the range of six or eight names. All this can take place in a matter of seconds.

This skill is used not only in finding telephone numbers or looking up words in the dictionary. It is used in scanning the newspaper for the information in which one is most interested, or in getting the necessary information from a recipe book, a technical manual, or even a scholarly book. An adept decipherer can even handle a multiple-choice reading test by using the questions and the scanning ability to answer the various items, without having to read each passage.

MEANING AND MAKING OUT
THE MEANING IN A TEXT

If there is a great difference between the skills required for our writer to produce legible text and those of our reader to decipher what she has written, does this same difference appear in the activities of producing a meaningful piece of writing and making meaning out of what someone else has written? At first glance, one might say that they are quite similar in that both the writer and the reader have to bring into play a large amount of the knowledge that they have in common. On the other hand, some fundamental differences exist between the decisions that writers and readers must make in order to make a meaningful text or to make meaning out of a text.

Clearly, a writer must first sort out what she is going to write about and decide in what genre, or type of text, she is going to write. At times, this decision is quite easy. Many times, furthermore, the choice has already been made for the writer. There are three major kinds of text that writers produce, depending on the demands that are placed on them: recording information, reporting, and exploratory discourse.

Much writing resembles some of the earliest forms of writing; it is simply *recording information.* We find this sort of documentative writing in laundry lists and telephone messages, as well as forms, checks, bills, certificates, and letters confirming conversations. In these kinds of writing, both the information and how it is organized are virtually established before writers even begin to write. All they have to do is fill in the blanks.

A second kind of writing is reporting. The information is known or easily available to the writer, but she has to organize the information herself, and she must select the style and tone in which to write. I call it *reporting* because the writer is a witness to the scenes, events, or ideas; her task is to find an appropriate style of text in which to place this information. Many of the narratives that people put into letters fall into this category, as do descriptions of people, places, or things that we observe. So too do minutes of meetings, reports of telephone conversations "for the record," business letters requesting something or explaining why the request cannot be fulfilled, and academic or scholarly articles. In most of these cases, the writer does not have to do much to get the information: It is known, it can be observed, and the limits of what is to be written are established by precedent. The real problem is putting it into a form that best holds and transmits the information.

The third kind of writing is that in which the selection of information and the form in which it is to be stored are both chosen by the writer. The writer must invent or generate the ideas, events, and scenes, and must choose the way in which to organize them, as well as the particular style and tone to use. The sort of writing that emerges is best called *exploratory discourse.* It includes most of the literary genres, but it also includes various kinds of reflective and theoretical writing. This essay would probably be so categorized, for I have had to come up with what I want to say as well as the way in which I want to say it. I have that sort of liberty in this particular task I have set myself, and it is a liberty I would have denied myself had I chosen to write a research report in applied linguistics. There I would neither have been able to indulge in the sort of speculation that I have been playing with nor would I have been able to select an organization and style that allowed for some of the sentences and paragraphs I have written.

The writer, then, selects or has selected for her the particular kind of writing she is to do. This selection includes choosing the particular function of discourse that will dominate the particular piece of writing, whether it is focused on the writer, the message, the reader, the language, the contact, or the world outside the textual one. Again, this choice is sometimes automatic, sometimes deliberate and freely entered into. When freely entered into, the choice is based on knowledge of what kind of text conventionally fills what sort of function and on knowledge of what limitations in information, organization, and style and tone accompany that particular kind of text. The choice is based on knowledge, and the choice activates that knowledge.

The choosing is a part of the planning that a writer enters into, and it may involve a long time or it may be semiautomatic. Clearly, people do not take a long time in planning what they are going to say on their Christmas cards or on their shopping lists. They may take as much as several years, however, in planning a major piece of writing such as a novel or a poem. People may also interrupt their writing to go off and think some more about what they want to say. The research on planning suggests that it is highly variable and individual. The poet Samuel Taylor Coleridge is said to have planned his poems while climbing mountains. His friend, William Wordsworth, planned his while walking round a small formal garden. I know people who like to do physical exercise as they plan, others who appear to enter trances, and still others who can write an extensive thoughtful essay with no apparent time for planning at all. In some cases, all the person's life up to the moment of writing has been planning for that writing.

When people actually begin writing, assuming that the writing is other than simply recording a telephone message or taking the minutes of a meeting, they then bring into play much of the knowledge about texts that they have acquired. In the actual course of writing, much of what people do is semiautomatic. Experienced writers do not really think about the spelling of words, punctuation, paragraphing, and grammar. All these have become part of that skilled or habitual text-inscribing capacity that they have. Their attention is directed primarily to what the words and sentences mean and how they are organized. There may be a moment's pause for a decision about a particular word or about whether to say x before or after y. For some writers there may also be a pause to check the spelling of a word or the grammar of a particular sentence. At times the writer may pause and go back over what she has written to check on what needs to go next; in other cases, she might rush ahead and write several pages without stopping or reconsidering.

During the period from the initial stroke of the pen or keyboard to the time when the writer says to herself, "There, I've finished," there may be a great deal of going back and forth over the text—or there may be virtually none. In part, the variation depends on the particular kind of writing task she has undertaken; a friendly letter may need less revision and polishing and going back and rethinking than would a letter of application for a job. In part, however, the variation depends on the idiosyncrasy of the writer, the way of writing that best suits her personality. As I initially drafted this last sentence, I noticed that I had inadvertently typed a second t on "the." I stopped to go back to correct it. Other times I have not bothered to stop to check or make corrections until the day after I have drafted a section. Why I do the one the one time and the other the other is somewhat of a mystery.

However I do it, I, like most other writers who are reporting or exploring in their writing, engage in the activities of drafting, or putting it down the first time; revising, or changing the sense or style or structure by adding, subtracting, or substituting words, phrases, sentences, or sections; and editing or polishing, making corrections of spelling, grammar, sentence structure, and in some cases neatness and penmanship. To a greater or lesser extent, each writer engages in these three acts (together with planning) whenever she engages in the activity of writing. The sequence, emphasis, or order of these acts is highly variable, depending on the writer's personality in conjunction with the situation in which she finds herself. Some writers, both professional and amateur, do not actually revise what they have written; instead, they may publish a piece and then sit down and write another version of it. To the dishonest among them, it is a way of making more money for a minimum of effort, but to the more scrupulous of them it is not a new work but a revision, or *reversion*, of the first work. These writers appear never to be satisfied with what they have written. They continue to reinterpret, and each time they appear to be saying to themselves, "This time I'm going to get it right."

This phenomenon leads to the question: "How does a writer know when she is finished?" The answer lies in the knowledge that writers have and employ when they write. From their varied experiences with different sorts of texts and genres, writers develop mental models of what texts of a particular kind "look like." An individual model includes most of the aspects of written discourse that we listed in Chapter 1. That is, on the basis of one's knowledge of the information contained in particular kinds of writing, as well as of the organization, language, style, tone, layout, and uses of that particular kind of writing, there emerges a model, or a template, of the final version of a specific type of text for a specific occasion. This model appears to control a writer's decision-making as she is coming to the end of the activity of writing a particular text.

In some cases, a writer may decide to violate the text model that is in her head. She may do this for effect, because she knows that others, particularly potential readers, share the model and so she wants to use that expectation against her text—or her text against that expectation. Other writers may also violate the model as part of a conscious effort to reform the genre or to rebel against the previous orthodoxy of writers in the genre. This shifting relationship between the writer and the model explains, as I have suggested, how conventions change and how the world of texts comes to have its own existence apart from the information it refers to and the individual writers who have created its various components.

If this set of activities and choices describes what writers do in the course of shaping the text as an agent of meaning, can I assert that readers work in the same way as they make meaning of the texts that are there before them? I think not. The reader is confronted by a text, not a blank screen or sheet of papyrus. Making meaning in written language is quite different from that of making out the meaning of a given text.

Like the writer, the reader has a number of choices to make, but the choices are not those of the writer. The first choice is that of how to approach the text. I said earlier that reading a text, like writing one, is a transaction between the individual reader and the printed page. As readers enter into the transaction, they may decide to treat the text as if it were providing them with information, or teaching them a lesson, or seeking to persuade them, or providing them with an aesthetic experience. In all cases except the last, each reader is expecting to take something away from the text. When I use the word "decide," I do not intend that every decision about how to read is conscious. People often pick up a text with a purpose and find that, as they proceed through it, their purpose shifts. At times they may simply pick up the text idly, to while away the time, only to find that they have found a purpose as they have gone through it. In many instances, however, the decision is conscious.

In aesthetic reading, the end is in the reading itself; it is for enjoyment or pleasure in the experience while the experience is going on. The decision to read a text aesthetically affects how we read, what we pay attention to. As I suggested in the discussion of the typographical error in the newspaper, had that word appeared in a poem that we had decided to read aesthetically, we would have assumed that the unusual character of the word in the particular context called for us to enjoy the image of "emasculating to violence," even if it might be somewhat obscure. By choosing the way in which we read, we decide to see the text differently, and we shift the focus of our attention from the information to the various devices by which that information is presented. The reader may take away information, or be persuaded, or feel he has learned a lesson, but that is a by-product of the experience. The reader's choice also has little to do with the purpose the writer may have had in writing the text. We can read an advertisement as if it were a poem. That is our decision even though someone may say that it is not an appropriate decision.

It is also true that the purposes that the reader sets out with may not be the ones he ends up with. He may begin to read a book with the idea of learning something, and end it with a sense of having been through an exciting experience from which he cannot mention a single specific that was learned. Furthermore, the reader may decide to shift the action he had originally proposed in response to the text. A reader may have opened a book with the intention of finding a specific item of information thought to be in it. Four hours later he could be writing an essay about the book and have completely forgotten what it was he was searching for.

As the purpose for reading shifts, so too does the expectation of what will result from the transaction. In some cases the activity of reading is primarily a search for particular items of information; in others it is a search for a generalized sense of the contents of the text. Beyond this search there can be such kinds of reading in which the reader interprets the text, criticizes it, and judges its value. Each of these kinds of subsequent activity can arise from an initial reading by which the reader seeks to take something away or seeks pleasure in the aesthetic experience of the text.

During the course of reading a text, a reader can, like the writer, shift actions either consciously or unconsciously. The reader can go back and forth in the text, turn back to reread a particular section, or move ahead to the end to determine whether the butler did indeed do it. This shifting back and forth can bring about a revision in the reader's understanding of the text, and it is a necessary part of the activity of making meaning of a complex text. Although it is a form of revision, it does not change the text, as does the writer's revisions, but it changes the conception of, or understanding of, or attitude toward, or experience of (or all these in combination) the text.

Although like the writer, the reader approaches a text with a model in mind, he uses the model differently. He uses it first to locate the particular text in his world of texts, to categorize the particular in a general framework. "Oh, I see. He wants me to. . . ." "Yes, this is simply a love story." "How nice of them to think of us; did we send them a card?" Each of these remarks and many others come from matching the text with a model of what texts "like that" are supposed to do or to be. The reader may reformulate his model on going further into the text, and the text, when it is read, becomes a part of the modification of the model for that particular sort of text that is in the reader's mind.

The model and the purposes of reading include, as I have suggested, not merely what may be thought of as rational or purely cognitive. They clearly include the emotional, so that we may read a particular text with the expectation that we will cry or that we may find ourselves laughing or being awestruck. The emotional reaction to a text is partly dependent on the text and partly dependent on the particular experiences of the world and emotional state of a reader at the time of reading. The emotional response to a text may vary considerably from reading to reading within a person as well as from person to person.

There is some debate as to whether these varied emotional responses to the experience of reading a text parallel the emotional state of the writer while she was writing it. In some cases, the writer may indeed be carried away to tears or laughter by what she has written. In many cases, however, the writer has detached herself from the emotional experience and may be coldly aware of the potential emotional effect of her text on its readers. For the writer, the emotional experience probably preceded the actual writing, which is, as Wordsworth wrote, "emotion recollected in tranquility," rather than the "fine frenzy" of the writer in the act of writing. Not so for the reader who comes upon the text, for whom the experience is, or can be, such that an emotional reaction to the text will emerge, even despite the reader's efforts to control himself.

The very idea of a reaction to a text, or what is referred to as a response to a text, forms the final aspect of the activity of reading and the final point of difference between reading and writing. To a certain extent it is possible to say that whereas a writer finishes writing, a reader never finishes reading. For the writer, once the information has been encoded, it is separate from her and she can go on to other things. She has gotten the information out of her system, although obviously a portion of it remains with her long after she has completed it. Not quite so with the reader, who picks up a text, decodes it, and makes meaning of it; that meaning remains within his memory as knowledge. Some texts are more memorable than others, and the human mind is quite good at purging, or at least suppressing, unwanted information.

At the same time, many of the texts that we read remain with us. As we read them and immediately thereafter, we may have a response to them: We may move about, cry, ponder the implications, decide that the text is worthless and the writer an incompetent fool, or make any one of a number of intellectual, emotional, or physical responses to the text we have been reading. This afterlife of the activity of reading has a vague counterpart in the writer's planning, but the resemblance lies only in the fact that either may take a long or a short amount of time.

As I have suggested in the first section of this chapter, the response to a text is in part the result of convention, in that we have learned that some kinds of texts are to be responded to by certain kinds of action; others are to be responded to with laughter or tears (at least that is what is expected); still others are to be pondered and argued about. In some cases combinations of responses may be expected. That we may be expected to respond conventionally does not mean that we will always do so; clearly, the reader is autonomous. He may groan at an anecdote or laugh at a romance. He may throw away an invitation. He may even write a critical interpretation of an advertising circular. That the reader may defy convention does not mean that convention does not to a certain extent circumscribe his responses.

Readers and writers, then, are bound together by the knowledge they share, about both the world and the world of texts. This textual common knowledge and conventional wisdom form the greater part of the compact by which the two are joined in the scribal society. Using this knowledge, they go their separate ways to inscribe or decode the information into or out of texts, making meaning or making meaning out of them. They have acquired both a great deal of knowledge and considerable skill that are at times quite esoteric and complex. How the scribal society trains, teaches, or educates its neophytes is the subject of the final chapter.

CHAPTER 5

Becoming a Scribe
and Other Unnatural Acts

In the past three chapters, I have set forth some of the principles of the world of written language and examined them from the perspective of history, philosophy, and psychology. I have advanced the notion that being highly literate, being a member of what I have called the scribal culture, involves awareness of the fact that written language is a system for storing information in visual space according to a set of conventions. This awareness is part of an ontological compromise that members of the scribal culture subscribe to, in which the text is seen as having a relationship to a nontextual world, being the product of a purposive intelligence called a writer, being related to other texts in a number of ways, and being capable of being interpreted by various readers in various ways. Operating within these constraints, writers and readers activate a great deal of common knowledge as they go about their separate activities of enscribing and decoding, making meaning and making out the meaning. Embedded in these principles is an assumption that there exists a distinction between the scribal world and the world of the merely literate. The scribal world includes that group of people who have created and continue to create "modern" culture, by which I mean culture that depends on written language and its capacity to foster scientific, technical, and certain kinds of humanistic and religious endeavor.

I will now address an aspect of the complex industrial world of literacy that has come to have a life of its own: the world of literacy teaching. All that I have described in the preceding paragraph is taught and learned. This world of teaching is almost coterminous with the term *schooling,* which is to say, the institutionalization of education. In many societies, young people move into the adult world within the confines of the home or the village. They are not sent to a separate educational institution. In other societies, however, there are separate places where young people go to learn the necessary skills of the adult world—hunting, husbandry, cooking, carpentry, and village life. These schools are removed from the adult village but somehow parallel to it and are directed to return people to the village life.

Schools in the scribal world are quite different. Their purpose is to take children from the family and the village and to prepare them to take their place in a larger literate society. This is "education." To a certain extent, it was always thus, although for many people becoming a scribe was a matter of apprenticeship in an institution like a monastery or convent; for many, particularly women, literacy was learned in the home. It was not until the printing press made the world of texts readily available that the idea of universal literacy, if not universal education, came into the human ken.

People often claim that education exists to "free the individual." I suggest that such freedom is illusory, for the scribal world demands that people surrender much of their freedom in order to belong to it. Only a few who have become the masters of the scribal world are "free" enough to change the conventions of the scribal world.

My purpose in this chapter is to shed light on the institution of scribal education. The "experts" on the teaching of writing and reading form a number of sects, not only in the United States but throughout much of the world. The various sects spend a great deal of time attacking one another, and their slogans sometimes appear ridiculous to the outside observer. "Process not product," "phonics is the salvation of reading instruction" (or its damnation), "holistic teaching," "grammar as the way to wisdom," "student-centered curriculum," "expressive writing," "creative writing," "instantiation of inferencing," "metacognitive awareness" are but a few of the current slogans that one finds in the world of language teaching. As with all slogans, these are but half-truths, and I urge those who are concerned less with bandwagons and more with the education of the young and inexperienced to be wary of every one.

Peanuts cartoon. (*Peanuts,* August 2, 1986. United Features Syndicate. Reprinted by permission of UFS, Inc.)

My purpose, here, is in part to outline what I see as rational instruction in reading and writing that would follow from what I have set forth in the preceding chapters, particularly Chapter 4. I remind you that there I referred to reading and writing as "activities"—that is, purposeful sequences of acts with the goal of effecting a change in the self or in the environment. Given such a definition, for example, one cannot consider processes without products, as Sally Brown well knows.

I begin the discussion with a definition of how one can define achievement in writing and reading in the scribal world, and from there I move to some of the necessary consequences of that definition for instruction. Finally, I state what I see as a likely sequence to the curriculum. I do not go into the niceties of instructional method. Although I subscribe in principle to the idea that teaching should be humane, I believe that the teacher must be seen as an authority concerning the scribal world. The teacher is not infallible, but the teacher should not feign ignorance or strive to be ignorant. The teacher must encourage a variety of approaches to instruction including the lecture and demonstration, discussion, laboratory work, group work, tutoring, and individual work, and should use all possible mechanical aids, from chalk to microchip.

READING AND WRITING AS EDUCATIONAL CONCEPTS

As I suggested in the preceding chapter, the concept of scribal behavior implies three interrelated facets: knowledge, text-enscribing activities, and meaning-making activities. One could turn these three facets directly into an educational program, for once one has a sense of the structure of a field, the reconceptualization of that structure becomes easier. Let us step back for a moment and consider educational goals and objectives, particularly as they relate to subjects like reading and writing in which knowledge, skill, and habit of mind are intermingled.

When one thinks of a concept such as school reading or school writing, it is sometimes best to begin at the end rather than the beginning. Rather than consider the child who enters the system, one can begin by thinking of the adult who emerges from it. Once one knows the destination, then one can consider the path. With respect to the scribal world, the fully developed reader or writer has developed a set of competencies and a set of preferences. As suggested in Chapter 4, for the writer the competencies include what we might think of as skills necessary to inscribe a legible text and those needed to produce meaningful discourse. In addition to knowing how to write, the writer has developed a set of preferences for writing fully developed texts, for writing a great deal, for writing in the appropriate tone or style, and the like. We may think of preferences as a combination of habits and choices. Good habits are desired ways of doing things, and good choices are the indication that one has the values and norms of the group. In writing and reading as in many other areas of human life, skill is matched by the willingness and even the desire to exercise it—but to exercise it in ways that are appropriate to the general or particular scribal pattern.

Achievement in writing can be demonstrated by the diagram on the opposite page which I sharpen and define in the next few pages (it proceeds from the general to the specific). The competence to produce discourse, as I said, clearly involves the writer's competence in making or managing the meaning in text. The writer must be able to generate or reproduce various ideas, images, observations, and memories; she must also be able to organize them according to a pattern appropriate to the general rules for structuring content. Thus, if the writer is dealing with several events, she must arrange them in sequence with the appropriate signals, which is the common method, or vary that arrangement, with sufficient cues for the reader to notice the variation. In addition to this cognitive competence, there is the social competence of using language and a general tone of address that conforms with the norms of the situation. A science report uses a different language from that of a letter to a favorite cousin. In addition, there is the pragmatic competence based on a knowledge of when what kind of writing is to be done and not on what a possible audience might expect.

This competence is matched by another sort of competence, that which is involved in producing a readable text. This involves text-related linguistic and graphic competence, and, when called on, the motor competence to use the necessary tools on the particular surface. The text-related competence includes competence with the grammar of the language, its spelling and orthography, and its various graphic conventions. All these kinds of competence mean that our writer has acquired and is bringing into play a great deal of knowledge about language, texts, and the ways of the scribal world.

When she sets about demonstrating her competence, the result is a text, which has features that can be observed and commented on. In general, observers of any text fasten on seven features:

1. The quality and scope of the ideas.
2. The organization and presentation of content.
3. The style and appropriateness of tone.
4. The grammatical features.
5. The spelling and orthographic features.
6. The graphics and layout.
7. The legibility and neatness of the text.

Bringing various criteria to bear, ranging from the highly personal and emo-

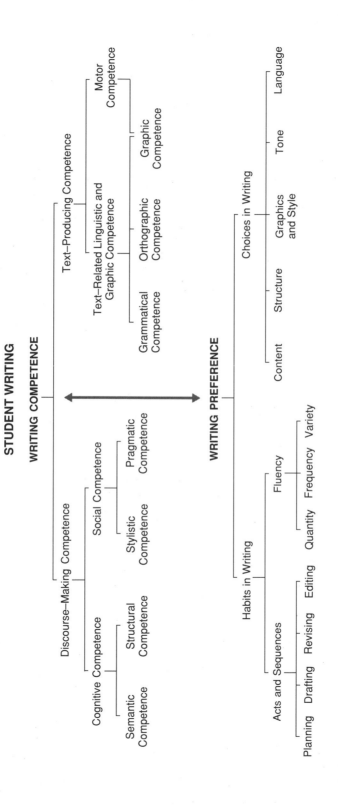

STUDENT WRITING

WRITING COMPETENCE

Discourse–Making Competence

Cognitive Competence
- Semantic Competence
- Structural Competence

Social Competence
- Stylistic Competence
- Pragmatic Competence

Text–Producing Competence

Text-Related Linguistic and Graphic Competence
- Grammatical Competence
- Orthographic Competence

Graphic Competence
- Motor Competence

WRITING PREFERENCE

Habits in Writing

Acts and Sequences
- Planning
- Drafting
- Revising
- Editing

Fluency
- Quantity
- Frequency
- Variety

Choices in Writing
- Content
- Structure
- Graphics and Style
- Tone
- Language

91

tional to those that are the consensus of the particular scribal community, the observers then judge some or all of these seven features of the text and by inference the competence of the writer.

These features also form the basis for an observer such as a teacher to make judgments about the writing preferences of a given student. Generally, these judgments are made over time because they require more than one sample of the writer's work. The preferences of the scribal society include that the writer make it a habit to plan her writing, check and revise her successive drafts, and edit the text before releasing it. The society also expects her to be fluent—to write frequently, particularly on demand, to write a sufficiency of text rather than the bare bones, and to write a variety of types of text as the occasion demands it. As to choice, she is expected to select topics, genres or text types, attitudes or tones, stylistic devices, and words and phrases that are considered desirable for the various kinds of texts she is called on to write. The student writer must be articulate, but at the same time must be fluent, flexible, and acquiescent to the norms of scribal behavior.

Thus far, I have been quite general. Can I be more specific about the various norms? In some respects I can, but in many respects the norms are determined by various subgroups within the scribal society as a whole. In the United States, for example, it is considered generally appropriate across subjects and fields of study for students to subscribe to the following 10 commandments:

1. Generally avoid the personal except in certain English courses.
2. If there is a choice between being abstract and being concrete, be concrete.
3. Use a propositional rather than an appositional structure.
4. Avoid metaphors and figurative language.
5. Generally avoid using graphic signals such as underlining, subheads, and the like except in science and mathematics.
6. Focus on the content rather than on making the reader feel comfortable.
7. Select a single aspect of your subject and announce your thesis as early as possible.
8. Make sure the surface appearance of the text is attractive. Check spelling, punctuation, and grammar.
9. Use complex or embedded sentences.
10. Avoid humor.

As I have said in earlier chapters, however, more specific norms are set by the various fields of study, business, and occupation. In elementary and high school and the early years of college or university, there is less specialization of norms than emerges later in advanced courses and graduate study. One of the reasons for this, I believe, is that many of the teachers of introductory courses are themselves not fully aware of the norms of their disciplines, or that there are norms. They will say that the students "can't write," and send them back to the English teacher who is also unaware of the norms of the other disciplines. That poor soul teaches the student that she should write like a student of English and the humanities, which is precisely what the science teacher does not want her to do. So she has to learn the science norms by trial and error. So it is in most of the fields of study in the United States.

If we turn to reading, we find a similar division of the construct of reading into competences and preferences, and these two are again divided into their subordinate levels. Meaning-making has its cognitive and its social aspects, and evoking text has its linguistic and its perceptual aspects. The cognitive aspect of reading is divided into an analytic aspect and an interpretive aspect. Readers should be able to analyze (or at least apprehend) the semantic aspects of a text (that is, what the words relate to) and the structural aspects of that text (that is, how the various parts are related). The interpretive aspect of school reading calls for the ability to summarize what a text "says" and generalize about what the text "means." It is here, in particular, that we see at work the practical compromise described in Chapter 3. The assumption of school reading in the United States is that a text says *one thing*—that its content can in fact be reduced to a summary or paraphrase to which there is universal assent. *Othello* is a play about a Moorish general who is tricked into thinking his wife is unfaithful, and so he kills her. Such an assumption makes testing reading easy. Some texts used in school reading programs allow for some ambiguity in interpreting their meanings. But even so, there is a set of interpretations or inferences of that text which is considered "reasonable." (See the diagram on page 94.)

Because a text exists in a social world for the reader as well as for the writer, the cognitive competence of the reader requires that he recognize the stylistic devices that are used and their intended effects. There is also the pragmatic competence of knowing how to treat the variety of texts in a world in which reading is at times to be responded to by writing a response, by ignoring the text, or by some other action or gesture.

To bring this competence into play, the reader must have the capacity to evoke a text in the mind from the marks on the page. Clearly, this competence requires visual acuity (or sensitive touch for those who read Braille). Equally important, the reader must use knowledge of various aspects of texts and text graphics in order to "decode" (as the reading specialists call it) the text. The reader usually employs one or more of three kinds of cues: (1) graphic cues that signal words, syllables, letters, or ideograms and their relationships according to the various spatial conventions prevalent in the culture; (2) already known whole words or ideograms; and (3) syntactic and

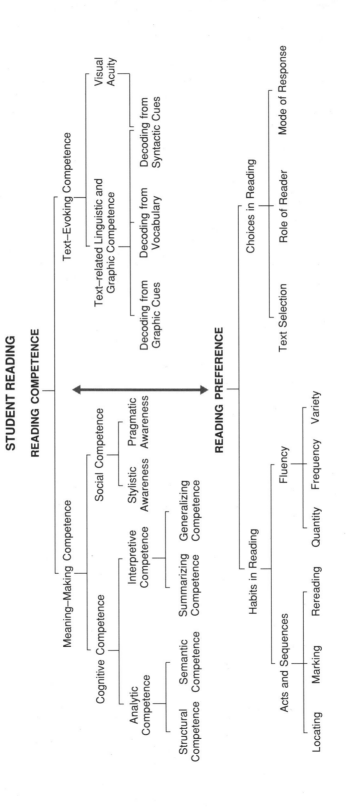

STUDENT READING

READING COMPETENCE

Text–Evoking Competence

Visual Acuity

Decoding from Syntactic Cues

Text–related Linguistic and Graphic Competence

Decoding from Vocabulary

Decoding from Graphic Cues

Meaning–Making Competence

Social Competence

Pragmatic Awareness

Stylistic Awareness

Interpretive Competence

Generalizing Competence

Summarizing Competence

Cognitive Competence

Analytic Competence

Semantic Competence

Structural Competence

READING PREFERENCE

Choices in Reading

Role of Reader

Mode of Response

Text Selection

Habits in Reading

Fluency

Variety

Quantity

Frequency

Acts and Sequences

Locating

Marking

Rereading

semantic relationships among words. Thus, the reader has three ways of decoding a word from its parts, its whole in isolation, or its place in a nest of words.

The preferences that a reader develops in the course of schooling may be seen as habits and choices. The habits involve sets of acts and their sequences—in particular, the acts of locating information, marking the text in an appropriate way, and rereading or changing pace when certain kinds of texts are presented to him for particular purposes. The fluent reader is marked by reading at an appropriate frequency a sufficient amount of textual material in a given amount of time, and by varying both frequency and quantity according to the demands of a specific subdiscipline. A fluent reader will take the same amount of time with four pages of mathematics as with ten times as many pages of history.

As far as choices are concerned, the well-schooled reader will select certain kinds of texts over others. He will prefer a "good book" to "trash." At the same time in some societies, he will also grant that trash is perfectly all right for others. The good reader will also select the appropriate role for reading certain kinds of texts as opposed to others. As suggested in Chapter 4, the good reader of fiction will set out to read the book with an aesthetic perspective and not read it as if it were a cookbook. The good reader will also respond to a text in the preferred manner. That is, say, the reader will talk about a particular text according to the fashion of his teachers. When reading a scientific article, for example, he will talk primarily about its content and its use of evidence and experiment, but he will not discuss the style or syntax of the piece. He may do so, however, if he is in a class in his mother tongue and the text is a poem.

To be more specific about the nature of school-based reading as it is taught in the United States, as a result of instruction, readers tend to obey the following precepts:

1. Read narrative structures with ease, and try to turn all other texts into narratives.
2. Produce accurate summaries that reflect the stipulated expert "meaning."
3. Locate information readily.
4. Do not reread, even if they like the book, except for a test.
5. Read quickly.
6. Read for recreation unless there is something on television.
7. Recognize "good" books but don't read them.
8. Do not read texts aesthetically, but read all texts as if they were scriptural (either divine or secular).
9. Seek the moral lesson in whatever they read.
10. Therefore, have a strongly censorious attitude toward books that are considered sinful or seditious.

The last four characteristics form a complex set of somewhat secularized preferences that have their history in the Protestant Reformation. This is the form of reading instruction from the very first grades in school.

The characteristics of the good school reader and writer taught in the United States are not universal throughout the world. Studies of comparative achievement and performance in reading, writing, and literature suggest that both in terms of aspects of competence and patterns of habits and choices students in various educational systems learn culturally appropriate patterns of behavior. Such a finding is not surprising, given what I have said in earlier chapters about the nature of the various scribal societies. They differ from one another; they are related to various cultural and religious beliefs and practices; and they tend to be conservative and self-perpetuating. Educational systems being what they are, they serve the goal of teaching children the norms of a society. Individualism is best developed in the light of those norms and outside the school system, which has a difficult enough time teaching the conventional wisdom that I have earlier described.

INSTRUCTION IN THE ACTIVITIES
OF THE SCRIBAL WORLD

If what I have described in the first section of this chapter constitutes schooling in the scribal society, how is a child led through the maze toward the destination? To most observers of schooling around the world, the answer is through trial and error. In most cases, instruction in reading and writing is unsystematic at best and haphazard at worst. It is for that reason that most studies of performance in reading and writing suggest that those who make it in the scribal world do so because of the accident of birth. Only in a developing country where most of the families are equally unschooled do children learn to read and write in school. To return to the two charts, research has shown that schools successfully indoctrinate students into the appropriate preferences but that they are less successful in developing the competence. In this section, I offer an alternative to the current practice, an alternative that is based on the preceding three chapters, in which I established something of the nature of texts and the scribal world. I believe that one can create a curriculum that is firmly based in theory and less hit or miss than is the present curriculum.

To begin, I believe that the best way to teach a subject is to start with the general concepts to be learned and move to the specifics. I also believe that it is best to be honest with students and tell them what one is doing and why one is doing it. Too much that goes on in schools begins with details and never gets to the general concept, and too much is shrouded in mystery. Beginning with the general and becoming increasingly specific follows the broad pattern of learning noted by psychologists as being most effective. Children's use of language begins with large categories like "doggie" and becomes increasingly discriminating. So, too, psychologists have found that people learn details better if they have a grasp of the whole; it's easier to think of a letter as a point in the alphabet rather than as an individual letter. Too much of current drill and most exercises in reading and writing are meaningless only because they are seldom placed in a context where they can have meaning. To provide context for scribal learning, students from the fourth grade and beyond should be shown the two diagrams explaining reading and writing as school subjects that appear earlier in this chapter to give them a sense of the domain and their place in it.

The curriculum in reading and writing should be constructed around the concept of text and the functions of text in the scribal society. Even young students should explore the world of texts much as I have explored it in the first three chapters of this book. They should find out what the various examples of texts have in common; how they are used in work, school, community, and home; and how they may change from society to society and during the course of history. The students should explore why texts have become so important and why they appear to dominate our environment.

During the course of this exploration, the students should read and write a great deal and should have available all sorts of texts, from comic strips to scientific articles, from advertisements to obituaries. This variety enables the students to acquire the various models of text that they need in order to be scribes in a scribal society. They need examples of the various things that they will be asked to read and write so that they can gain a sense of the content limitations, structural properties, and stylistic characteristics of the genre, or type, of text.

To some persons it might seem that an emphasis on text as the central organizing principle of the curriculum is misplaced, that I should focus instead on reading and writing, and thus center the curriculum on human acts and experiences. I certainly agree that much of the curriculum should involve these acts and experiences, yet it seems to me that one cannot get the proper breadth or perspective on what one is doing unless one has a sense of why or to what end. The student and the teacher need a map, that is, a concept of the field. For reading and writing, the most encompassing concept is the text, for it involves, as said in Chapter 3, the reader and the writer as well as the world of texts and the world outside of texts. I also think it important to have the central concept to be a noun about which verbs can move, and an entity outside of the students so that they can contemplate something besides themselves. Only a text has an objective existence, and texts contain more than the individual human can know. Even as ordinary a text as a telephone directory exceeds the capacity of the human mind, as do most texts, despite the fact that they are produced by humans. Practically speaking, having the concept of text as the center of the curriculum means that the students can have a sense of having learned something, of having mastered some content, not simply of having pursued a mechanical skill like touch typing. The various lessons and exercises that are assigned can then fall into place indeed.

I also believe that it is clearly important for the students to gain familiarity with the world of texts, and particularly with those texts that their culture values. In that way, they can become at least passive members of their culture and develop some sense of participating in an entity and having continuity with the past. Left to their own devices, people today will cleave to the sets of "classics" of their peer group and particularly to those selected and promulgated through the media, thus remaining merely literate. The schools tend to err in seeking to incorporate this media culture into the curriculum. Generally a "popular" text enters the schools only as it is on the wane, and these texts are often resented by students when they are brought into class. A better strategy is for the school unabashedly to limit itself to what the scribal society has called *classic* rather than what the media advocate as the current fad.

Recently some "experts" on the curriculum have rejected these classic texts as being too difficult, boring, and irrelevant. That need not be the case; it depends on how these texts are treated. I agree that some of the classic texts are difficult, but many are not. I am not suggesting that first-grade students be told to read *King Lear*, but they might well read or have read to them the major folk tales of the Brothers Grimm or the stories of Hans Christian Andersen and Hergé or the poems of Laura Richards and Eve Merriam. Some students in the upper grades of secondary school or the first years of college or university should be expected to read Shakespeare and Dostoevsky. By then, these texts would not be difficult, and there is no need to make them difficult by insisting that the students come up with the interpretation agreed on by a group of middle-aged scholars.

It has generally been my experience that those students who find these texts difficult also find them boring and irrelevant, but when the classics are properly presented most students find them to be both interesting and timely. To be sure, the poems of William Wordsworth that deal with middle age are not likely to stir the soul of a teenager, but one does not have to insist that students read those particular poems. I suspect that many students find these poems boring and irrelevant because their teachers are not particularly interested in poetry and use anthologies that tell them that only the more esoteric symbolic interpretation is the correct meaning of the text.

A curriculum based on the concept of text would involve the students in many activities related to the production and reception of texts. They would do a great deal of writing and reading. It is clear that one can become a competent scribe only through practice. The nature of that practice should include focus on the constituent competencies that I have listed as well as on the broader activity of writing or reading a complete text. The psychological concept of an activity that was discussed in the Chapter 3 suggests that when one undertakes an activity, one has a purpose or an end in mind. The activity encompasses a number of discrete acts, and these acts often include subsidiary operations. To give an example, when a writer is producing a text on a word processor, mental attention is focused on the semantic, structural, and stylistic aspects of the text. At the same time, she is writing words with correct spelling and punctuating those words in an acceptable manner—all this with little direct awareness. She may stop to think about the spelling of a word or she may decide that a comma is better than a semicolon in a particular place. If a specific program is on the word processor, she may have to stop to use the proper commands for underlining or italics. Once, each of these acts and operations constituted a distinct conscious activity in its own right. At one point, she painstakingly learned the alphabet and the shaping of the letters; now that has become automatic, as has much else that she now uses in the course of writing her text.

Many pedagogues spend a great deal of time attacking workbooks and exercises and are currently inveighing against the extension of them into computer-assisted instruction. Their attack strikes me as similar to an attack on a music student's practicing scales or on a mathematics student's calculating sums. Many of the acts that constitute reading and writing need to be learned to the point of automation. The only way to do this efficiently is through practice. I agree that nothing but dull practice indeed makes for enervating teaching and resistant learning, but in moderation practice is needed on such subskills as decoding, forming letters, spelling, punctuation, preparing summaries, writing openings and closings to stories, creating metaphoric versions of texts, and putting words together in various patterns. All these subskills and more have their place in the total instructional picture, and they must be practiced. Many forms of practice can be enjoyable. A teacher can use "Mad Libs" to have students practice parts of speech, rhyming contests for decoding, the game "Hangman" for spelling, and the like.

In writing practice, writing openings and closings, a description without adjectives or adverbs, or a paragraph of minute detail or one using extended metaphor can be treated like finger exercises. None of these is to be confused with the larger purpose—text.

Another one of the vexing concerns in relation to the curriculum in reading and writing is the extent to which the students should learn conventions and rules rather than be encouraged to be freely creative individuals. The focal point of much of this concern is the issue of grammar. Many people argue that student writing would improve if only they knew and studied grammar. Others say that the teaching of grammar has no effect on the quality of student writing so that it should not be taught. Most of the studies that lead to this conclusion have examined the teaching of grammar as a logical exercise and found it to have little relation to ratings of the cognitive competence as displayed in texts written by students. Other studies have shown that when students try to extend their grammatical and syntactic competence through practice, there is indeed the effect of improving the grammar of the texts and their semantic and structural aspects as well. Grammatical competence forms a starting point for writing although it is clearly not all of writing, as some people once seem to have thought. People use grammatical knowledge primarily in text producing and editing; it plays little part in producing discourse.

Much of this debate, however, misses the central issue. What is attacked is form because it is presented apart from the functions of discourse and text. Form follows function and should be approached through function, not divorced from it. In any scribal culture, grammar, like spelling, punctuation, and the structure and organization of various texts, constitutes one of the sets of conventions that are used by readers and writers in storing and recovering information. These "rules" are generally agreed to as matters of convenience to those who use written language within a society. They are necessary parts of the model building that needs to take place so that both the reader and the writer can operate in the world. It is also important for readers and writers to have a firm grasp of these conventions so that their deviations from them become a matter of purpose, not of naive error. The formation of portmanteau words like *brillig* and plays on syntax by James Joyce, e. e. cummings, and Lewis Carroll can only be seen as effective examples of art because the reader and those authors share the conventions that are being violated. (See the poem by cummings). Just so with the student writer. She can, as I just did, get away with that bane of language teachers, the sentence fragment, only because she has assured her readers that she knows she is violating the convention.

Convenient conventions are an important part of being a scribe, and I would not deny this knowledge to students, but I would explain just how and why they are conventions and what purposes conventions serve. Students in the United States should learn the structure of the overused and overabused "five-paragraph theme," precisely because it is a useful conventional method for organizing many different kinds of reports. It states its point directly, supports it with a sufficient number of examples to constitute acceptable evidence, and it modifies or restates the main point in the light of that evidence. It is the structure of much of science reporting, which advances a hypothesis, presents the evidence, and then affirms or refutes the hypothesis. It is a useful tool, although it is not the only way of organizing information to make an effective report. Its virtue is its illusion of objectivity. It is inappropriate for the presentation of subjective experience; that misuse is what makes it anathema to English teachers.

```
snow)says!Says
over un
        graves
                der,speaking
(says.word
Less)ly(goes

folds?folds)cold
stones(o-l-d)names
aren'ts

)L
   iv
es(c
      omeS

says)s;n;o;w(says
W
I

elds)
un
   forgetting
                un.
der(theys)the

:se!crumbs things?Its
noyesiyou
he-she
(Weres
```

Poem No. 34. (From *no thanks* by e. e. cummings. New York: Liveright Press, 1935. Reprinted by permission.)

Another bone of contention relating to the teaching of such matters as grammar and literature in the forming of the scribal society concerns the extent to which students should learn the terminology of that society. Cannot one be a good scribe without having to know all those words—*sentence*, *noun*, *metaphor*, *plot*, *passive voice*, *setting*, and so on? The answer to that question is: Perhaps, but knowing them helps. The reason that it helps is that such terminology helps teacher and student communicate about the various texts that surround them. It also helps in the communication among scribes in various roles such as author and editor, or reader and lexicographer. Such terms serve the world of the scribe, just as musical terms serve the musician or composer. They permit discussion about the various texts and their parts to move quickly and conveniently; such terms allow people to perceive the connection among texts more readily. Such terms are not the whole of instruction in being a scribe, but have a function.

The issue is not whether to teach grammar or nomenclature but how to teach them. One bases the curriculum on text and approaches text by looking at the functions of text—how texts are used by writer and reader. Then, one can argue that form follows function, as just demonstrated with the five-paragraph theme. It is a form that follows from a function. So too is a sentence, a modifier, a setting, a metaphor. They should not be taught simply as forms but always placed within the context of the functions of text. They cannot usurp the place of the texts in scribal activity or scribal pedagogy.

A curriculum based on the concept of text, therefore, allows students to understand their role in the scribal society. It allows them to become more than literate, for they are privy to much of the mystery that seems to surround the world of the written word as it has grown. Such a curriculum focuses on the activities of reading and writing and seeks to develop the competence and preferences of the students within the confines of the scribal culture, and to allow the opportunity for them to modify that culture. It does so by giving them the requisite knowledge and the power to employ it in the complex world of the text and the scribe.

THE STAGES OF THE NOVITIATE

Having set forth what I see as the components of a possible curriculum that devolves from the concept of text, I add some notes concerning the sequence that might best help a child who has little but an intuitive sense of the world of texts progress toward being a full scribe. In most of the industrialized countries and in many of the developing nations, sighted children can hardly help but notice the existence of print and texts. They are ubiquitous and have even become a necessary aspect of underwear, even if the texts are in a foreign language—usually English. The young child is perhaps most aware of the pictographic nature of texts and will often acquire a sense of the meaning of a whole logograph such as the front of a cereal box or the sign of a fast-food restaurant. Early "writing" often has the outward appearance of text, much in the way of Saul Steinberg's cartoons.

It seems possible, then, that early literacy instruction should capitalize on this sense of the visual and on the *gestalt* of texts as conveying part of the implicit message. Such an approach would complement the attention paid to the relationships between sounds and their visual counterparts—letters, syllables, and other markings. One obvious way into the world of printed words is through a medium of the comic strip or comic book, which is to a great extent logographic in character and which has developed and adapted a set of conventions of which many young children are aware. The four-panel strip is

(From *The Passport* by Saul Steinberg. New York: Random House, 1974. Re-printed by permission.)

also a good introduction to the conventions of the fictional story with its rising action, climax, and denouement—as the selection from *Peanuts* that appeared earlier in this chapter testifies. In fact, the ability to order the four panels according to Western narrative traditions is often seen as an indication of intelligence. Both taken as a whole and examined with an eye to its constituent symbols, the comic strip provides an easy introduction to the concept of visual convention that is intrinsic to the world of text. One can move from that to the various other formats and conventions of text that surround the child, such as the sections of the newspaper or the telephone directory.

Another side of introducing the child to the functional and formal consideration of the world of texts appears when one considers the sorts of texts that are to be read. In many parts of the world, the child in school is presented with a diet of stories and narratives, either fictional or factual, that are usually somehow "graded" as to difficulty and readability. Often, too, the texts are rewritten to make them easier and more "available" to children. As suggested in the previous chapters, the variety of text types is large, and although the story is one of the older oral forms and a form certainly available to most children, I do think there can be too much of a good thing. It has been my experience in working with children as they learn to read and write that they can and do like to read a variety of texts. If a child is really interested in how locks work, that child will want to read something that tells how locks work. If another child wants to read about pirates, that child will not settle for a watered-down version. In the United States, a steady diet of basal readers is not sufficient fare for children whom one wants to become more than literate. The basal readers may even inhibit budding scribes.

The curriculum of text should include real books written by real authors and written in a variety of genres. These texts should not simply be narratives but should include works organized according to the major structuring principles: the sequence of time, the sequence of space, and the sequence of classification. The sequence of time includes narrative but also descriptions of processes from boiling an egg to playing a complex game like "Dungeons and Dragons" to assembling a computer. In its most elaborate form, the sequence of time involves discussions of causality and multiple causality that one finds in scientific and historical writing. The sequence of space includes descriptions of physical objects and places as well as of various artifacts of increasing complexity from the description of a room to the description of the biosphere. The sequence of classification involves the separation of objects or ideas from one another to show their commonality and individual nature. Classifications include definitions and, in their most elaborate form, they also include comparisons and contrasts that explain the minute details of the similarities and differences among events, things, and concepts. I have discussed earlier the various everyday manifestations of these sequences, which form the basis for most Western texts from cookbooks to treatises on abstruse economics. It is important that children be exposed to these sequences throughout their schooling.

Therefore, those planning a curriculum that focuses on the idea of text should make sure that students have access from the beginning to a variety of real as opposed to regurgitated texts that illustrate the main text organizations as well as those that exemplify the purposes and functions of written language and those that express discourse-making demands. I have discussed that variety in Chapters 3 and 4. Children should be made aware from an early stage that the world of text is a rich one indeed.

As I said earlier, it is important for children to be exposed to the classics of the scribal culture and not be presented with only the latest and newest. To understand contemporary texts readers need to have at their mental fingertips certain of the texts of the past. For students in the United States, I would begin the sequence with folktales and myths of European and Middle Eastern culture and supplement those with folktales and myths of the African, Indian, Sino-Tibetan, and Native American cultures. I would not omit the literature of the major religions. I would introduce early some of the classical works for children such as the writings of Louisa May Alcott, A. A. Milne, Mark Twain, Laura Ingalls Wilder, and E. B. White. To these I would add such poets as Langston Hughes, Christina Rossetti, and Robert Louis Stevenson. During the course of the primary school years, children could build on these beginnings with a program of broad reading, including such volumes as Lamb's *Tales from Shakespeare* and Stevenson's *Treasure Island* as well as the writings of some of the more modern European writers like Tove Jansson and Maria Gripe, both of whom are unfortunately little known in the United States. I would hope that the children would be exposed to and encouraged to read a variety of works, some of them individually, some of them in large or small groups. Some they may not like, some they may find use stereotypes. But these stereotypes are no greater or less than those used by Carolyn Keene or Judy Blume. To accomplish this goal, teachers even through the eighth or ninth grade should spend about 15 minutes a day reading aloud to the students. In that way even those who have trouble disentangling the world of print have access to the texts that will help them when such troubles are overcome.

Not all the texts should be fiction or prose. Text should include poetry, drama, and a variety of classic nonfiction such as historical texts, personal essays, and expositions of scientific and other issues. There is no reason why children in primary school should not be able and encouraged to read something of such writers as Xenophon, Livy, Bacon, Parkman, or Lewis Thomas. Not all the works of each of these writers is easily available, but if the selections that are available are not badly mangled in order to make them readable they will be useful. It is my experience that if children are engaged by the substance or style of the text, they will make extraordinary efforts to work out the difficult bits.

The sequence of the curriculum should be controlled by the nature of text and its relation to graphic and other conventions as well as to the variety of text types and their relation to the broader culture from which they come.

In addition, the sequence will inevitably move, as said in the first section of this chapter, from an emphasis on those aspects of the activities of reading and writing that concentrate on enscribing and decoding activities to those that concentrate on discourse or meaning-making activities. Such a sequence, however, should not be so rigid that there can be no meaning-making until after all the skills of text enscribing have been mastered. Although the first can build on the second, it is not appropriate to argue that an individual cannot master the first until the second has been thoroughly learned and codified within the memory. Even young children do make meaning out of what they write and do intend to make meaning when they write. The execution may be more faulty than the intention, but one should not deny the intention.

At the same time, it is true that young children do not make the same meaning out of the texts they read that adults do. They tend to view stories and poems and plays more personally and more viscerally. They are not the detached spectators that adults are. Such personal interpretations and judgments can be developed, strengthened, and supported through a schooling that does not insist that children come up with adult interpretations but does encourage students at an early age to expand and explain and, to the extent that they can, justify their responses to what they read.

As they engage in talks about what they are reading, children can also begin to enter into the sort of discussion about the ontology of text that was discussed in Chapter 3. Even a young child can begin to explore the extent to which printed words, like their oral counterparts, are arbitrary signals of concepts, objects, and events. Children can also begin to explore the extent to which a text can be reacted to or interpreted variously, and they can learn the distinction between the text and their personal reaction to it. The easiest way to introduce this concept is through the joke. Why is it that some people laugh and others don't? One may also move from a joke to a fable or to an ambiguous story such as Frank Stockton's "The Lady or the Tiger." The relationship of text to object can be seen easily in the variety of signs and notices that cannot be taken literally (such as an ad that reads: "Wanted concrete sidewalks . . . Please call . . . "), as well as by the discussion of what changes are made in a word or sentence when it is manipulated graphically or syntactically. The relation of text to text can be illustrated with stories that use direct allusion to such texts as nursery rhymes and with folktales that are often retold and changed as they move from culture to culture. Each of these is an introduction to the nature of texts and the ways they are used and considered in the scribal society.

Finally, the curriculum should introduce to the student a goodly amount of what is known about what we do when we read or write. Children should be introduced to the idea that they must know a good deal if they are to be successful writers. They must be disabused of the notion that writing and reading are equated with decoding and penmanship, spelling, and grammar—the current view of about four-fifths of the American people (and people in many other societies). The importance of the various kinds of knowledge must be stressed, and it can be done easily by asking the children to consider what they do know when they look at particular texts. They can also be asked to attempt to read scrambled texts or to write the same information in various genres to see how it can be changed. They can even be asked to read a text that deals with something beyond their range of knowledge and talk about why they cannot understand it (the text may deal with a different culture with different norms and procedures).

It is important to stress the role of knowledge and to explore with the students what they do and do not know when they begin to read and write, and how they might go about supplying the missing knowledge. Equally important is to have the students explore their own capacities and activities as they go about text-inscribing and text-decoding. It is also important for them to be conscious of their own mental and physical processes. Even though many children begin to read or write using a microcomputer, they should experience what it is like to make a woodblock or linoleum block text, what it is to use pen and ink. They should even, I think, spend some time practicing calligraphy to get the sense of accomplishment that comes from creating a physically appealing text. They can also use their word processors to explore computer graphics *and what they might* do to make the text readable, noticeable, or simply strange.

Novices in the scribal society should also be made as conscious as possible of what they are doing as they enter into the transactions of meaning-making and making out the meaning of the various texts they read. To call attention to what they are doing will at times slow the students down at that particular moment, but they should be aware that text models exist in their minds and in the minds of their writers or readers and that the two do not necessarily match point for point. Having realized this fact, they can then begin to see that they can make choices. As it is now, many students bounce from class to class, each time being told "This is what a composition [or an interpretation] is, and there is to be no deviation." Although teachers have the right of authority in the classroom, a petty tyrant simply discourages the student. The introduction to what it means to be a scribe and to make scribal choices can begin relatively early, as with the choice of whether to send a sentimental or a sardonic greeting card and a consideration of how the one or the other will be read by people like grandparents, relatives, or comparative strangers. The choices of genre and interpretive stance are already evident at this level.

I have been suggesting in this section that one can introduce children at a very young age to the nuances of the scribal society, and that one should do so consciously in order both to capture the interest of the children and to help ensure that more of them will become full scribes.

THE GATEKEEPERS OF THE SCRIBAL SOCIETY

One other issue is related to the education of the scribal society: the nature and sorts of gates through which people must pass as they progress toward full membership. These gates are visible as examinations of one kind or another, measures of past performance and purported predictors of future performance. There are also invisible gates, such as race, social class, and language background, but the visible tests are often surrogate measures for making sure that the current scribal society maintains its particular nature. Race, social class, and especially language background are linked to being a scribe, because by the very definition of a scribal society (a definition that the society has made for itself), scribal behavior implies certain boundaries to the appropriate dialect of the appropriate language and the appropriate cultural knowledge. In the United States, for example, such limits are currently those of Standard Written English and the culture of the Judeo-Christian or Western heritage. This general depiction is modified for the person who wishes to become a member of a specialized group such as the scientist, accountant, advertising executive, or bureaucrat. The scribal world is not democratic, although opportunity to enter into the competition may be equal.

The visible tests form an integral part of schooling in scribalism, and they appear to be as necessary today as they have been from time immemorial—or at least to the tests on the Torah or the Chinese civil service examinations of 1000 B.C. To be necessary is not to be just, of course, and although I might argue for the abandonment of tests, I shall not. The scribal society is limited in size and, by its own definition, has become highly specialized. The tests that have come into existence in this century and that echo those of earlier centuries have sought to differentiate the literate majority from the scribal minority.

I have argued in the previous sections of this chapter that it may be possible to educate more scribes through certain practices that to me seem common-sensical but that others may see as Quixotic. At the same time I argue that there need to be some modifications of the tests and gates that currently surround the inner temples of the scribal society. One reason for this argument is that a great deal of public money as well as a great deal of time is being wasted on tests that could be better used in practice and learning. Although it is clear that there probably should be gates between common schooling and secondary schooling (at least to help students see how well they might fare in a more "academic" program), as well as between secondary and university schooling, I am not sure that there should be standardized norm-referenced tests of language performance every year during primary and secondary education. These tests serve primarily to allow real estate salesmen to raise the prices on the properties in those areas where the schools have higher scores. They are seen as representing the world of texts and are texts themselves. Their scores are seen as indicating literacy and scribalism.

I am quite sure that these typical standardized multiple-choice tests that are currently so popular in the schools and with school boards are about as poor an instrument for determining the potential for being a scribe as could be devised. Such tests, which claim to measure reading and writing and whose results have immense power in determining an individual's future, barely touch the range of competence that constitutes being a scribe. For the most part, they cover only the text-enscribing and text-evoking aspects of competence. They do so for the simple reason that these two aspects of the tests represent the limits of multiple-choice testing. It is difficult to create solid reliable tests with only one right answer when one is concerned with meaning-making or making out the meaning and when one deals with preferences. As I have been constantly suggesting in this book, the issue of right and wrong becomes blurred when one considers the nature of text and the activities of the scribal society.

To return to the two diagrams that appear in the first section of this chapter, I invite you to consider a question: What qualities and abilities must students manifest to satisfy a gatekeeper that they are ready to pass through a particular gate? I do not intend to become technical about this issue but to suggest certain general principles and to raise certain questions.

To take reading first, it is important for students to demonstrate that they are able to read a variety of texts in a variety of genres. Although it may be that there is a general index of reading performance that is readily tapped by a vocabulary test, I am not convinced that such a test can show whether students can read, for example, both a poem and a technical manual. We need to know if the students are aware of the different ways by which meaning is made in the two genres. Any measure of reading should include a variety of texts, not all of them sustained prose, and it should also include some complete texts, rather than the contextless sentences and paragraphs that pervade American tests. The test questions should cover the various competences I have listed (semantic, structural, stylistic, pragmatic, grammatical, orthographic, and graphic). In addition, there should be some measure of the students' reading habits and choices, which may give an observer a good means of predicting whether a particular student should be encouraged to become a scribe.

Similarly, in writing, it is clear that students must be tested on their competence to produce texts and discourse; the test must require the students to write something. Experience shows that it is not enough for a student to write a single composition in a period of some 20 minutes to be judged competent. That is but one kind of writing. The students should be required to write a variety of types of text, from the pragmatic to the reflective and argumentative. Their texts should to be scored by trained raters for the degree to which they demonstrate the range of competences.

DIMENSIONS OF A WRITING ASSIGNMENT

A. Instruction
1. Topic only
2. Topic and content cues

B. Stimulus
1. Unspecified
2. Word, phrase, or sentence
3. Text (non-literary)
4. Text (literary)
5. Photograph
6. Music
7. Other media
8. Realia (field trip)
9. Mixed

C. Cognitive Demand
0. Unspecified
1. Reproduce facts
2. Reproduce ideas
3. Organize, reorganize events
4. Organize, reorganize visual images, ideas, etc.
5. Invent, generate, evaluate

D. Purpose
0. Unspecified
1. To learn
2. To convey, signal
3. To inform
4. To convince, persuade
5. To entertain
6. Multiple

E. Role
0. Unspecified
1. Write as self (journal, monologue, etc.)
2. Write as self (autobiography)
3. Write as self (detached observer)
4. Write as other (assumed persona)
5. Write as other (detached author)

F. Audience
0. Unspecified or teacher
1. Self
2. Specified individual (addressee of letter)
3. Specified group
4. Classmates
5. General public
6. Other

G. Content
0. Unclassified, multiple

1. Self
2. Family, relatives, home
3. Peers
4. Specific individual (non-literary)
5. School, schooling, education
6. Leisure activities (sports, hobby, reading)
7. Community
8. School subject: mother tongue, literature
9. School subject: other
10. Social, political, cultural, economic issues: general
11. Science, man and nature, ecology: general
12. Psychology, philosophy, religion, ethics: general
13. Other

H. Rhetorical specification
0. Unspecified or multiple
1. Note, informal letter
2. Formal letter (e.g. business letter)
3. Resume, summary, paraphrase
4. Narrative
5. Description
6. Exposition, analysis, definition, classification
7. Narrative, descriptive, exposition, with evaluative comment
8. Argument, with evaluation and comment
9. Literary genre
10. Advertisement, media
11. Journal writing

I. Tone, style
0. Not specified
1. Overall tone, style specified
2. Particular stylistic devices specified
3. Overall tone and style and stylistic devices specified

J. Advance preparation
0. None, unspecified
1. Class discussion
2. Group discussion
3. Collecting materials
4. Previous work studied

K. Length
0. Unspecified
1. One paragraph ($<$ 150 words)

DIMENSIONS OF A WRITING ASSIGNMENT (continued)

    2. 2-5 paragraphs (< 2 pages)
    3. 2-5 sides (300-700 words)
    4. > 5 sides
L. Format
    0. Unspecified
    1. Specified as to use of space on page
    2. Specified as to conventions
    3. Other specifications
M. Time
    0. Unspecified
    1. Impromptu (< 30 minutes)
    2. Impromptu (30-59 minutes)
    3. Impromptu (60-120 minutes)
    4. Impromptu (> 120 minutes)
    5. With pre-writing activities (< 60 minutes)
    6. With pre-writing activities (60-120 minutes)
    7. With pre-writing activities (> 120 minutes)

    8. Impromptu homework
    9. With pre-writing homework
N. Draft
    0. Unspecified
    1. One draft only
    2. One draft with corrections
    3. Rough draft and revision with second copy
    4. Rough draft and revision to final edited copy
O. Criteria
    0. Unspecified
    1. Grammar and orthography primarily
    2. Style and appropriateness primarily
    3. Organization and presentation primarily
    4. Ideas and content primarily
    5. Neatness primarily
    6. Combinations of above
    7. Other criteria

(From "Towards a domain referenced system for classifying composition assignments" by A. C. Purves, A. Soter, S. Takala and A. Vahapassi. Research in the Teaching of English, 18 *(4), December 1984. Copyright © 1984 by the National Council of Teachers of English. Reprinted by permission.)*

The approach to testing that I propose is expensive, I realize, but not out of reach. Its most important result would be that the *norm-referenced* test so overused today would no longer be used. By norm-referenced, I mean a test that is simply an assembly of questions only roughly approximating a domain of learning. Such tests are given to a group of students on the assumption that their performance will be distributed along a normal curve. Then it is said that the average score is the norm for the age or the grade group, and that anyone who falls below the average is a poor performer. The score says nothing about how well students can read or write or whether they are fit to go on to the next stage of the novitiate.

Just as the curriculum should represent the domain of scribal behavior, so should the various tests and gates. This sort of test is called a *domain-referenced* test. It makes sense, for it forces the test-maker to seriously consider the nature of the domain and the markers of effective or satisfactory performance within that domain. Having defined the variety of constituent competences that underlie the concepts of reading and writing, the test-maker could now come up with the specifications for a test or series of tests that would represent the domain and at the same time be fair to the student. The exercise of moving from the sort of diagrammatic view of writing or reading to specifying the tests and submeasures and how they would be marked and scored is a lengthy process. It can and should be done by those who intend to set the standards and guard the gates.

An example from an earlier work indicates what might have to be considered when a test-maker writes the assignment for a test of writing. Each of the items in the table on pages 110–111 needs to be addressed so that the test-maker can ensure that the assignments from year to year will be comparable. We know that if one were to attempt to write assignments that represented each of the combinations on the list, the task would involve some 30 billion years, assuming the rate of one a minute. The point of such specification is to enable the test-maker and the educational policymaker to be sure that two tests are equivalent.

In testing writing, there is not only the setting of the question to be considered but the grading of the composition that results. As the table shows, such grading should not be a single score but should include separate scores on the various aspects of the composition that indicate the particular competences. It may be that one composition should be scored primarily for one competence, but to be fair to the students as well as to help them become aware of the complexity of the activity of writing and the world of text, one should score at least the following so as to cover both text-enscribing and discourse-producing competences:

- Quality and development of ideas.
- Organization and presentation of content.
- Appropriateness of style and tone.
- Grammatical competence.
- Spelling competence.
- Handwriting and neatness (if appropriate).

The persons grading the compositions should be allowed to indicate the extent to which they as readers are attracted or repelled by what they read. This need not be reported to the student, but my experience tells me that such a rating helps graders to be more objective about the other aspects of a composition.

The parenthetical "if appropriate" after handwriting and neatness is inserted because in many scribal societies there is already a tendency for much writing in school to be done on a word processor. If students have become accustomed to such electronic assistance, they will be hampered by having to take a test using pen and paper. To do so would be like asking students trained in the use of ballpoint pens to write their examinations with dip pens and inkwells or chisels and stone tablets. While it is easier to make the format of the text attractive with a word processor, I do not think that students should be penalized if they do not have access to a word processor. I expect that more and more writing examinations will be of such nature that students can prepare the text on a word processor and that certain aspects of grading it can be handled with a computer program.

As with writing tests, so with tests of reading: Those who create the tests need to specify the variety of texts to be used. Variety can be defined in terms of field or area of content, genre or type of text, style and tone, as well as historical period, country of origin, and author. Each of these suggests a potentially limitless selection and variation. Beyond the selection of the text, there should be a selection of the kinds of questions that will determine whether the students can "read" the passage. The questions could deal with decoding, locating information, summarizing, generalization, interpretation, and evaluation. In the case of the last three, the issue for the examiner is whether the students come up with appropriate generalizations or interpretations and, even more important, whether they have learned the rules of evidence by which the scribal society accepts or rejects generalizations.

For both reading and writing, then, the tests that constitute the entryways into the scribal society need to be much more fully and carefully explicated than is currently the case. Beyond that, these examinations and their nature should be explained to the teachers and the students involved. The curriculum and the test should be related to each other, and I see nothing wrong in teaching to the test. If one does not teach to the test, then one is denying students the opportunity to learn that which they will need to have in order to go through the entryway. Such behavior on the part of teachers is morally indefensible.

Part of the testing system should involve questions relating to the nature of the scribal society, so that the students and their teachers can be sure that the curriculum involves not simply blind drill but conscious awareness of why it is both groups are doing what they are doing. Such a curriculum and its testing program should, in general, be better than the haphazard curriculum that exists today because they are rational and rationalized, broad, and as humane as they can be in giving as many people who want it the opportunity to enter the scribal society.

SCRIBAL EDUCATION AND DEMOCRACY

One nagging question remains: Has the curriculum I have proposed in this chapter really addressed the issue I raised in Chapter 1 of this book? Will the curriculum be any better than what already exists in attracting the minds of those who in the present scheme of things become severely disaffected? I do not know. It seems to me that the social problems of teenage pregnancy, drugs, crime, and—above all—poverty cannot be answered by the educational system alone. As many have observed, we do not invest our social capital in these people but prefer to let them shift for themselves, and many of them emerge from adolescence on the fringe of society. They are what we now call the underclass. Some are employed; some not. Some are successful financially; some not. Some are honest and upright citizens; some not. Most of them are not what we would call scribes, and they are often the dupes of those scribes who are less than honest.

Many of these people are referred to as illiterate. That term probably does not apply, for they can read, but they cannot or do not read and write sufficiently well to enter the scribal society. Could they have done so had their education been different? We cannot tell. We know that they are alienated from the educational system; either it failed them or they chose not to let it have its effect. For some the genesis may lie in their social class or racial backgrounds; for some it may lie in their family's negligence; for some it may lie in their peers; for some it may lie in the values promulgated by the media; for some it may lie in the deeply rooted anti-intellectualism of the United States. All these forces reinforce one another.

One thing is clear: Those who are scribes see education and scribalism as an avenue leading to economic success. This view is not held by many of those who are not scribes. Extrinsic and future gratification is not the most effective form of motivation for education; it should be intrinsic and present.

A curriculum that is based on the idea of text can be intrinsically motivating and interesting. It is a curriculum that begins with the textual environment of the child. It immediately seeks to help children make sense of what surrounds them, of what they can create and what they can comprehend. It is a curriculum that aims to bring more children into the scribal community, and it does so by being interesting and direct about the environment, by being honest and aboveboard, and by being supportive and challenging. It does so by asserting that there are rules and conventions. It does not lie to children about their uniqueness and creativity. It allows children to be full players in the literacy game. Such a curriculum may provide the opportunity for some of those who are at risk of being disaffected to enter into the scribal society. It will not be the same for all children; it can easily be adapted for the children of poverty and the children of immigrant parents, just as it will have to be adapted for the children of the suburbanites and the children of the rural communities. As a central generating principle, however, the idea of text has a better chance of being successful with more people than have some of the previous controlling ideas like "language arts," "reading, writing, speaking, and listening," and "growth and process." Concerning the textual world and the scribes who inhabit and control it, honesty is the best educational policy, as with all else.

An Afterword
on Thanks and Sources

The idea for this volume lies in a request from two of my former students, Gail Hawisher and Anna Söter, that we collaborate on a volume on literacy. This request was based on discussions the three of us and others had been having over two years concerning various issues related to literacy, particularly writing. I then went off on a Fulbright to Finland. Having little to do on the weekends, I started writing to my wife, Anne, a long essay on my views of literacy and explaining the research in which I was engaged. This essay proved to be not only my contribution to the planned volume but Gail's and Anna's as well.

The first draft was completed in six weeks. It was read and commented on by several people including Gail, Anna, and Anne, Sauli Takala and Anneli Vähäpassi of the University of Jyväskylä, Finland, and C. H. Knoblauch, Judith Langer, and Sean Walmsley of the University at Albany. I hope they can see their influence on my thinking. The revision I made was read by Naomi Silverman of Longman who had enough faith in it to send it out for review. To her and to the reviewers as well as to the production staff at Longman I am grateful.

My son, Theodore Purves, has done much of the art in the volume. Thanks.

In one sense this volume's genesis lies in the very first publication I was commissioned to write, an article for the Columbia University *Alumni Magazine* in 1961 on why college students could not write well, "The Dictaphone or the Pen." In it, I explored the differences between oral and written language. That essay was noticed by Alfred Knopf, who asked me to expand it into a book. I tried, but I soon realized I did not know enough; fortunately so did Mr. Knopf. I suspect I have been reading, studying, thinking, and writing in order to fulfill that obligation. This is the book I did not know enough to write in 1962.

Much of this book comes from a panoply of sources, some of which are fugitive quotations or snippets from my reading going back to my childhood interest in books and art; some are from a variety of conversations I have had with colleagues around the world; some are from various reconsiderations of my own research in the teaching and learning of literature and writing around the world. Instead of the normal array of footnotes and bibliography, I am going to cite a few of what I think are the key references for readers to pursue. The bibliography is selective, personal, and idiosyncratic. Anyone who is upset about being omitted is in excellent company.

Readers should by now have noticed that I have sought consistently to refer to the single writer as *she* and the single reader as *he*. Some might find this arrangement awkward, but it seems to me a good solution to a failure in our grammatical system.

CHAPTER 1

A number of works provoked this chapter. One of them is the discussion of the performance of United States students in tests of reading and literature, completed in 1980: A. C. Purves, D. Quirk, and B. Bauer, *Achievement in Reading and Literature: The United States in International Perspective*, Urbana, IL: National Council of Teachers of English. Other works that have been influential include Neil Postman's 1985 volume: *Amusing Ourselves to Death: Public Discourse in the Age of Show Business*; Richard Hofstader, *Anti-Intellectualism in American Life* (1963); E. D. Hirsch, Jr., *Cultural Literacy* (1987); and a variety of reports on adult and workplace literacy, including *The Subtle Danger* (1987), published by National Assessment of Educational Progress, and Jonathan Kozol, *Literacy in America* (1986), the Department of Labor's *Workplace 2000* (1987), and Daniel Wagner, *The Future of Literacy in a Changing World* (1987). The work of Shirley Brice Heath, particularly *Ways with Words* (1981), has clearly influenced my thinking about the phenomena of which I treat, even if I take a different tack from hers.

CHAPTER 2

The two main sources for this chapter are Arthur Gelb's *A Study of Writing: The Foundations of Grammatology* (1963), and Albertine Gaur's *A History of*

Writing (1985). To these one must add the works of J. H. Goody, particularly *The Domestication of the Savage Mind* (1977) and *The Logic of Writing and the Organization of Society* (1986); S. H. Steinberg's *Five Hundred Years of Printing* (1961); Jonathan Logan's *The Alphabet Effect: The Impact of the Phonetic Alphabet on the Development of Western Civilization* (1986), which is an extension of the work of Marshall McLuhan, particularly *Understanding Media* (1964); and of course, the work of Walter Ong, particularly *Orality and Literacy: The Technologizing of the Word* (1982). To these one must add Will Eisner's work on the visual aspect of writing, *Comics and Sequential Art*, 1985.

CHAPTER 3

For me, one of the seminal books in the area of readers, writers, and texts is Meyer Abrams's *The Mirror and the Lamp* (1953), which sets the terms of the debates that have raged in the past three decades. I have also been profoundly influenced by I. A. Richards, whose examination question in 1950 I am still trying to answer. It was "Once you have all the facts, what else do you need to criticize?" Other books dealing with critical issues that I have found particularly illuminating include Morris Weitz's *Hamlet and the Philosophy of Literary Criticism*, Northrop Frye's *Anatomy of Criticism* (1957), Jonathan Culler's *On Deconstruction*, Terry Eagleton's *Literary Theory: An Introduction* (1983), and, of course, Louise Rosenblatt's *The Reader, the Text, and the Poem* (1977).

CHAPTER 4

Any work on the psychology of literacy must be indebted to the work of Sylvia Scribner and Michael Cole, whose *The Psychology of Literacy* (1981) has caused a revolution in the ways in which we think of the activity of being literate. Their work is based on that of Vygotsky and his followers. To these, I would add the work of Roman Jakobson, particularly his work on the functions of discourse. E. D. Hirsch, Jr., *Cultural Literacy: What Every American Should Know* (1987) has had an impact on my thinking, particularly the idea that cultural knowledge forms a major part of the psychology of literacy, as has the work of Stanley Fish and his *Is There a Text in This Class?* (1982), which says much the same as Hirsch in a diametrically opposed fashion. I am also indebted to a vast array of experimental and speculative literature by many of my colleagues, particularly Linda Flower, Judith Langer, Arthur Applebee, C. H. Knoblauch, and Lil Brannon.

CHAPTER 5

My thoughts on the teaching of literacy are profoundly influenced by the work of A. J. Markova, whose *The Teaching and Mastery of Language* (1980) is perhaps one of the most important books of this century on language teaching. It is unfortunately too little known in the United States, in part because it is not easy to read, in part because it deals with the teaching of Russian, and mother-tongue teachers around the world are remarkably ethnocentric. To me, the other important writers on language pedagogy include James Britton, Gunnar Hansson, James Squire, Mina Shaunessy, and, on evaluation and assessment, Hildo Wesdorp.